You are FREAKING AWESOME

Waking Up to the SECRETS You already Know

Huni Hunfjord

Copyright © 2018 by Huni Hunfjord

You are FREAKING AWESOME

All rights reserved. No part of this publication may be reproduced, distributed, or transmitted in any form or by any means, including photocopying, recording, or other electronic or mechanical methods, without the prior written permission of the publisher, except in the case of brief quotations embodied in critical reviews and certain other noncommercial uses permitted by copyright law. For permission requests, write to the publisher, addressed "Attention: Permissions Coordinator," at info@BeyondPublishing.net

Quantity sales special discounts are available on quantity purchases by corporations, associations, and others. For details, contact the publisher at the e-mail address above.

This book is a work of non-fiction, based on the author's reality and adapted from the author's life purpose walking program Focus Gym Be you! and Focus Gym Walk the Talk, for this book.

Orders by U.S. trade bookstores and wholesalers. Email info@BeyondPublishing.net

The Beyond Publishing Speakers Bureau can bring authors to your live event. For more information or to book an event contact the Beyond Publishing Speakers Bureau speak@BeyondPublishing.net

The Author can be reached directly HuniHunfjord.com
BeyondPublishing.net/AuthorHuniHunfjord

Manufactured and printed in the United States of America distributed globally by BeyondPublishing.net

New York | Los Angeles | London | Sydney

ISBN 978-9-935937-100

THANK YOU, *You Are Ready!*

You just made this book real when you picked it up and started reading it. That is one of the many things that makes you freaking awesome! You are a pure creator!

I can't wait to share with you how truly amazing you are.

I understand if you don't feel like you're that awesome right now. I know that feeling well. I was there for a very long time myself.

All you must do is to trust me a little bit, empty your glass, and read with an open mind. After reading and implementing some of the very easy-to-follow exercises, you will be, act, and walk vibrating at a frequency I like to call *freaking awesome.* These exercises should be taught in every school.

Once you realize that people in control do not want you to know how super freaking awesome you are, you can start ignoring the social programming going on and start stepping into your born destiny of greatness! Yes, that's right: you are already freaking awesome! I am only going to help you remember a few things about yourself on this journey. You are ready!

WHERE TO FIND
Awesome Stuff About You

Thank You, You Are Ready! — 03
01. Be You — 07
02. Leader — 17
03. Lucky — 25
04. Outstanding — 33
05. Bob — 41
06. The Future Now — 51
07. The Dream Came True — 61
08. Superstar — 73
09. Good News — 87
10. Listen — 99
11. Lobster — 111
12. Obsessed — 123
13. We Are One — 133
14. Energy — 145
15. Your Garden — 157
16. Master — 167
17. Collective Beliefs — 179
18. Memory — 193
19. Witness — 207
20. Purpose — 223
Bon Voyage — 236
The Author, Huni Hunfjord — 237

01

BE YOU

> *Congratulations, you are now doing something that very few are doing!*
> **You are taking initiative!**

YOU ARE AN AMAZING PERSON!

Do you know how truly amazing you are right now? It does not matter whether you know it or not. You are here, you are taking initiative, and right now, you are the person that many look up to, because you are taking action. You are here and completely in the present moment, being you in the now. You are you, and nobody in the world can experience exactly what you are experiencing right now.

YOU ARE UNIQUE.

Have you ever heard the same story being told over and over again and perhaps, heard more than one person tell you the same story? When the same story is told by different people, the story gets a new perspective, because different people have experienced different things in life. The story will never be told exactly the same way by two different people. You experience the story based on your experiences. You experience the story differently than anyone else. You have been through many different things in life, and because you are a very unique person, you are the only one who can tell the story exactly like you tell it. The same applies to the experiences you will manifest while reading this book. You experience it in your own unique way! Your way!

You want to become a better person today than you were yesterday, and that is one of the things that make you so unique and awesome. I know this because you are here reading this right now. That tells me that you know deep inside how amazing you are and that you are ready to step into the best possible version of yourself. You are so ready to remember how truly powerful and magnificent you are.

Now, bring your attention to your surroundings. Notice all the things that are surrounding you right now! Look at something you've seen before, and concentrate on noticing something new about that thing, something you have not noticed before.

Do this now!

Are you inside or outside?

Do you see grass? Maybe trees, flowers, or plants? What about houses, cars, or people?

Try to spot something new in your environment right now!

What are the colors like in your environment right now? Are they bright, or are they dull?

How is the brightness where you are at now?

Do you see any signs of the seasons? Is there snow outside, or is everything about to bloom?

Are the trees blooming, or are they preparing for the winter?

Look at how the grass has been moved or how it got to grow and flourish without interference or care.

Do this now!

This is a very simple exercise that forces you to be totally present in the moment. Well done!

The soil is so important; it nourishes so many things. Did you know that you can influence the soil? By thinking beautiful thoughts towards the grass or the trees or the flowers in your home, you influence them in a positive way! Anything you think about affects the environment. You are so powerful that just positive thoughts can massively impact your environment.

You can affect the growth, and you can affect people in the same manner with your thoughts and your emotions.

You are a very influential person, and as soon as you focus on beautiful and happy thoughts and think about how beautiful life really is, you start to see the beauty in all the things that are in your reality. In other words, you will start to experience all the beauty in everything you see, touch, taste, smell, and hear. You affect it all by simply shifting your focus on the beauty of life, and there is plenty of beauty in it. All it takes is one decision. Decide to start noticing them.

Now, notice how you are breathing!

Are you breathing slowly, or are you breathing fast?

Are you taking deep breaths or shallow?

Are you breathing through your nose or mouth?

Now, only use your nose to breathe!

Now, only use your mouth to breathe!

How you breathe is so important! Be completely in the present moment, and feel the difference when you change how you breathe.

Do this now!

There is a big difference for your health how you breathe.

Now, feel how you are spreading all that oxygen throughout your body as you breathe, and how your body benefits when you consciously breathe a little bit deeper.

Try it, and feel the difference!

Do this now!

Now, if you try breathing only with your nose, what can you smell?

What do you smell?

Put your attention on experiencing and feeling how the oxygen you just inhaled into your lungs is being pumped throughout your entire body! Feel how you are nourishing your entire vehicle right now — your body, mind, and soul!

Now, try to hold your breath for a few seconds, and feel how that affects your body.

Now, breathe deeper and feel how the oxygen increases your concentration and how the oxygen nourishes your body, just like the soil does for the grass, trees, and flowers.

Are you smiling right now?

Go ahead, smile!

When you smile, remarkable things happen in your brain.

SMILE!

When you use the muscles in your face to smile, regardless of whether you have a reason to smile or not, your brain sends out chemicals that make you feel better. The brain does not know whether you are really happy or not. The brain knows that when you use those muscles in your face when you smile, it should pump out hormones throughout your body and make you feel better.

Today, you can find doctors who are recommending that people who suffer from depression simply look in the mirror and smile. This is not just a theory; it's known that a smile can do a lot for a depressive person — more than many drugs can do. This does not mean that they stop using prescription medicine — this means that with smiling as a ritual, a part of your daily tasks, you will be able to slowly decrease your prescription intake, and with other exercises, you can completely stop taking them, with a doctors consent, of course. No matter how you feel today or how healthy you are, if you take one to five minutes each day to just smile into the mirror — to smile at that wonderful human being who is smiling right back at you — you will feel better.

REMEMBER TO SMILE,
BECAUSE YOUR SMILE IS SO POWERFUL.

The next person you see — even a stranger — smile at them!

Do you feel what's going on in your body when you smile without a particular reason to smile?

Now, just take a few seconds and smile into the air — smile at the universe! Trust the process — smile like you just won the lottery, like your dream just came true. That's it; you got it!

It is amazing how much impact such seemingly small action can produce.

YOU ARE INCREDIBLY POWERFUL!

Did you know that it is possible to measure how high your energy vibration is right now?

When you smile, it increases the vibrational frequency you send out, and it increases your energy. Therefore, you have a greater impact on your environment while smiling.

Have you ever walked into a conversation where other people were laughing and having fun?

How did it impact you? Did you smile? Did you get happier? Did you smile before you knew what they were talking about?

Have you ever laughed and had the effect on others that he or she began to smile, or even laugh? It's a wonderful feeling to cheer others, isn't it?

What do you consider funny?

Do have something that brings you joy every single time? Do you have someone or something in your life that makes you smile every time you look at them or it?

Add that which gives you joy to your day today.

What is that thing that you have in mind right now?

Is it something you can watch on your TV or computer, or, even better, is it someone you can go and see later today?

Pay attention how your body reacts the next time you laugh. Put all your focus on experiencing how the brain reacts by sends out chemicals and hormones that make you feel great to your entire body. Be in that moment, and enjoy being you, because you are absolutely freaking awesome!

Now, focus on your shoulders!

Notice how you are carrying yourself right now. How are you sitting or standing?

Now, take a deep breath, and open up your shoulders.

Yes, just like that. That's great!

Now, imagine that you just accomplished something you have been dreaming about. Now that you have already done it in your mind, experience how you feel.

YOU FEEL GREAT, DON'T YOU?

Now, open up your shoulders even more, straighten your back and walk or sit like you image you will, once you accomplish that goal or task you have in mind right now. Open your shoulders and feel how you become lighter knowing you have already accomplished this goal and how gravity pulls less on your body. Feel yourself becoming lighter.

Experience how that feeling spreads all over your body.

Feel how great of a person you are. You did it. You made you dream come true! You are completely in the now. Experience how great you feel right now, now that you have accomplished this dream. It's complete; it's real. It does not matter whether you know how to accomplish what you are thinking about right now. The only thing that matters is that you can imagine how you will feel once you have accomplished it!

Wow, outstanding! You are a natural at this! You just created this!

Have you ever had a dream that was so real that you thought you were actually experiencing it, until you woke up? Your subconscious mind does not know the difference between a dream and being awake, and that is why the dreams can feel so realistic. You can trick your subconscious mind to experience how you feel right now, already having accomplished your dream. You have accomplished it already, now experience it.

By experiencing how you feel once it's done with your emotions, you have raised your energy vibration, and people, things, and opportunities start to present themselves in your reality to make this accomplishment a reality. This is how the world really works.

You're creating a new future — a better future — by experiencing how you feel right now with that thing already accomplished. Having achieved these goals or tasks already, no matter how big or small they are. You have accomplished it already. You did it.

Congratulations!

YOU ARE FREAKING AMAZING!

How do humans create anything?

Every single thing in this world that humans have created started as an idea, as a thought. They imagine their outcome as it being already done or accomplished, just like you have been doing right now.

You are a very powerful creator!

You are part of something greater than just you!

You are absolutely amazing!

Now, put your hands up above your head into the air, just like a runner who just won a race would do. Stretch your arms up into the air as far as you can reach.

Put the book down, and do this now for a few seconds!

Celebrate!

That's awesome!

This is you, celebrating that you did it already. You have already accomplished your dream.

You are truly awesome!

Enjoy being you in the now. Soak in what you have just read, and just be you! Practice experiencing as many wins as you can. Experience the greatness within you, and turn on the unlimited creative power that resides within you right now.

You have been absolutely amazing during this first chapter on your journey of stepping into your greatness.

This moment right now is so great, just like you are!

Put the book down for now, and just focus on enjoying the moment. Experience how great you are, right here, right now!

02

LEADER

> *I want to start this chapter by congratulating you for being you! You are back at it!*

YOU ARE FREAKING AMAZING!

You are no longer just taking initiative. Now, you are becoming a leader!

You are becoming a leader by taking the initiative again and again and by continuing to read and being you!

Those who are the most successful in life are the ones who take initiative again and again, just like you are doing right now.

YOU ARE INCREDIBLE!

You are setting an example for others to follow, to look up to and to learn from!

If you know that if 10 of your friends are watching what you do on a regular basis, you can multiply that by 100 to get a realistic idea how many are really watching you directly or indirectly right now. You are amazing. You are so influential that people are following you to learn from you and be inspired by your actions.

Do you have a hard time believing that?

Well, it's not so unbelievable. How many times have you looked at social media, read articles, or seen people and not told them you just saw them? It's normal. Everyone is doing it. Whether it's through their windows, from the car, through other people, or on social media, we have eyes everywhere. You are positively influencing a lot of people right now!

YOU ARE FREAKING AMAZING!

Your positive energy is positively impacting your environment and people around you right now!

If you are a woman, you are born with incredible power of creation that no man can ever come close to, or, for that matter, ever truly understand. You can create life! How much creation really dwells within you? Truth be told, the power you possess to create is beyond what you or anyone else can ever truly grasp.

This power within you has no limits!

This power to create is your gift, your birthright! Not only to create life, but to create so much more than that, because this creative power is not limited to creating life. Your creative power is only limited by you.

Not being able to conceive a child has nothing to do with the creative power a woman possesses.

If you are a man, you are born with the gift of being a leader and a protector, and your strength is beyond what you will ever truly understand. You truly have no limits, except the ones you put on yourself.

Everything you can think of, you can create! You can easily create long-lasting effects on your environment with your thoughts, emotions, and actions. Remember that the better you feel, the higher your vibration is, and the bigger the impact you have on your environment.

Today, place your attention upon something positive you have created by simply being you. Is your friend still asking for the same hairstyle you complimented a long time ago, or are your colleagues still doing something that was your idea or doing something that you did and they noticed and started doing themselves? Notice something positive in your reality today that you have created just by being you.

The next person you meet today, concentrate on finding something about that person that you can compliment that person on.

You look amazing today!

You have a very pretty smile!

Wow, those shoes look so good on you!

You are glowing today. Whatever you are doing, keep it up!

Your hair looks amazing!

Every time I see you, you make me feel great.

Is that a new coat? It's amazing; where did you get it?

You look so confident!

I love seeing you smile, because your teeth are so beautiful.

Have you been working out? You look fantastic!

You have beautiful hands.

There is something so special about the way you carry yourself that I noticed it right away.

You look like you are in a good mood. Now, I am in a good mood, too. Thank you!

You can always find something to compliment other people on. You are a very creative being!

Concentrate. Think and feel how wonderful you are right now, and remember to smile — it looks so great on you!

NEVER FORGET HOW POWERFUL YOUR SMILE IS!

Take some time now and just smile. While you hold that smile, feel how the power within you is ready to be unleashed.

Do this now!

You could power a whole city with all the energy inside of you right now.

Everything you put your focus on grows. That does not mean it grows in size, but it gets multiplied or magnified. If you concentrate and focus on how wonderful you feel, you feel even better. If you focus on pain, it gets worse. So, if there is anything that comes into your reality today that you do not want to magnify, ignore it. Don't give it your attention. If you have pain anywhere in your body, you can unleash the creative power within you by thinking about how your body felt in that specific location when it was healthy, before the pain. Let's use a headache as an example. You can focus on finding where it's located in your head, and when you have located the pain, remember how you felt right there before they pain started. When you succeed in remembering that feeling of being healthy, you have tapped into the creative power within, and your body starts performing a series of events that lead to changing your current situation into something better. Yes, that's how powerful you are!

When you get a thought into your mind that you do not want to magnify or manifest, just let it pass through, in and out. It's not yours unless you give it your attention.

Now, put all your focus on one of your thumbs. Do not think about anything else, just your thumb.

Think about what's happening inside of it by focusing on it. Keep your concentration on it, feel it, and be it.

Feel how it reacts when you move it a bit.

Feel how the nerves take the messages from the brain and send it all the way down to your thumb and it moves slightly. If you concentrate long enough on your thumb, you can start to feel your heartbeat inside of it.

Now, put the book down for a few seconds, and put your attention completely on your thumb. Sit still and allow yourself to become one with your thumb, feeling and experiencing the now in your thumb, totally in the present moment! When you get totally focused on it, close your eyes and keep feeling it, the heartbeat inside of it.

Do this now!

Did you feel your heartbeat in your thumb? Of course you did, because you a freaking awesome!

Did you notice that even though all your focus was on your thumb, you could continue to breathe? You blinked your eyes. Your heart kept on pumping, and a million other things were taking place in your body, even though your focus was completely on your thumb. You could have done this while walking as well. Even with all you focus on your thumb, you would have kept walking with ease. All these actions are controlled by your subconscious mind, and you don't need any focus to control these actions anymore, because they are automatic now.

If you focus on being happy or more cheerful with your conscious thought over and over again, eventually, your subconscious mind will take over and make it automatic for you. Your subconscious mind will take over any tasks you want to become automatic. That is why you don't have to focus on your heart beating, walking, moving your hands, riding a bike, driving your car, or breathing. Your subconscious mind knows you want it.

The subconscious mind simply says:

Okay, I got it. You can now focus on something else!

You don't have to focus on walking — not today anyway — but do you remember how hard it was in the beginning? Have you recently seen a baby learning to walk? Don't you think it's amazing how long it takes to learn, but, then, when you finally get it, you don't have to focus on it at all anymore? You can do this with anything else you want in life. Can you imagine watching a baby falling for the 25th time and thinking to itself, *Oh, I guess this is not meant for me*, and just quitting? Of course not. Remember this: you are still that child, and no matter what you want to learn today, you can, if you just keep trying.

Do you want to feel better or to be happier or even more cheerful? Focus on that. Focus on it consciously over and over again, until your subconscious mind steps in and says:

Okay, okay, I got it. You want to be happy all the time. Now, let me take over, and go focus on something else.

It takes time to focus on something often enough for the subconscious mind to realize that this is not a temporary situation or effort on your behalf, but a lifestyle change, like reading, for example.

You are incredible.

You are the most perfect creation of all time. Your body is much, much more powerful than you will ever understand. Your body and mind can accomplish things you might consider impossible today, but, with practice and the right mindset, you will learn how to unleash this unlimited power within you. Your journey has already started!

We are all connected.

We are all part of the universal consciousness — what is sometimes called collective consciousness. You receive messages from the universal consciousness daily. For example, when you know who is calling before picking up your phone or when someone knocks on the door and you already know who it is, or when you think about someone and later find out that he or she was thinking about you at the exact same time. You can also receive answers and get new ideas from the collective consciousness, and that might be the reason why when people get a great idea, about 50 other people in the world are getting the same idea.

The person who implements the idea first is what separates him or her from the others. When you are completely in the present moment creating something, painting, writing, playing music, or anything where you are completely zoned out, you are directly connected to the universal consciousness, and you can download freely as you wish. You can allow yourself to be in perfect flow with it, and that is often when the magic happens. Just like how this book was written.

Have you ever had an epiphany? Have you ever had such a great idea, all of a sudden, that you said to yourself: *Where did that come from?*

Where do you think it came from?

The universal consciousness is a big part of why you have such a great impact on your environment right now!

YOU ARE FREAKING AMAZING!

You are a part of something greater than just you. You are awesome, and you are unique!

Now, raise your hands above your head, up to the sky. Stretch your fingers up towards the stars.

Then, make a fist, and open your palm up again with all of your fingers pointing up to the stars.

Do this three times, now!

This is you celebrating that you did it. You are now becoming a leader. You are setting an example for others to follow! You are celebrating how magnificent you are right now! Congratulations on being you!

Put the book down for now, and use the time to reflect on what you just read. Focus on being you right now in this present moment!

Enjoy feeling and being the amazing person you are right here and right now!

03

LUCKY

> *What's up?*
>
> *I'll tell you what's up: you are, and you are awesome right now! You are active, and your performance is outstanding. You are keeping yourself on track. You have permission to be extremely proud of yourself, right here and right now.*

Can you feel the positive effects in your body from the oxygen you are breathing when taking a little bit deeper breaths?

You are treating yourself like a champion. Right now, you are treating yourself with respect and improving your well-being.

Well done!

The next time you walk, pay close attention to how your hands swing while you walk. Notice how your right hand swings in sync with the left leg and how your left hand swing in sync with your right leg. Then, put your attention on both arms, and feel how the swing as you keep on walking. Completely focus on your arms.

Go ahead and stand up and walk a few steps before you continue and see how this works.

Do this now!

Today, you are going to learn a little secret about how to walk a bit faster than normal. Not really fast, just a little faster than normal. Do you know the best way to walk faster? You keep on walking and focus on your arms. Hold your attention there, and try to swing your hands a little faster and a little further than usual and see what happens.

Do that now!

Did you notice what happened, especially what happened with your legs? Did you walk a little bit faster?

It is very likely that it happened automatically. This is something athletes learn to do, in order to run faster. They learn to swing their hands faster and further, and then, they start to run a little bit faster. It's amazing how sometimes you must implement a very subtle change to do a lot more. That applies to so many things in life; it's often a little change that's needed to create the change you want and crave.

Your body is amazing! Your body is perfect. Have you ever looked at your body and noticed something you have not noticed before? This may not have happened recently, but certainly at some point, you did notice something new on your body, something you had not noticed before. When you see or learn something new in life, it broadens your horizon. The new part or thing you noticed, can no longer be unnoticed. It's something you will always see from that day forward; it has changed your reality. The same thing happens to you when you learn new things or do something new for the first time; it becomes your new reality.

When you get a new car, for example, you will start to notice the same kind of car you are driving in your town, driving on the streets. You notice that there are more cars just like yours on the street that you did not see before you got the new car, yourself. A woman who becomes pregnant or starts to crave having a baby suddenly starts noticing how many women are pregnant all around her. Her focus is on something new, and that's what she notices all around her, in her new reality. The same can be said for people who learn how to spot business opportunities. As they are learning how, they go and practice looking for opportunities, and they suddenly start to see opportunities everywhere. When you learn to cook for the first time, you will start to notice new things on TV or on the Internet or even in the kitchen at your friend's house. This is because everything you put your attention on grows. Your attention to similar or identical things is amplified, and then, your reality is changed.

When I talk about your reality, I am referring to everything you see, hear, notice, feel, and everything you believe. Do you have something that happens all the time in your reality? For example, when you are driving to school or work, do you always get a parking space? When you go to the store, do you always tend to start a conversation with someone? When you hurt yourself, are you are always quicker than others to heal? Do you always get better grades than others when you are studying something? The reason for these recurring events in your reality is simply the fact that you know they will happen. This is your reality; it is your reality because, at some point, you have decided that this is so, and your attention is focused on those expected results, and therefore, they keep on repeating themselves in your life. Have you started to notice more people reading since you started to read yourself? Is there anything else you have recently started doing and now, you notice how many people are doing the same thing?

Is there anything you want to change in your life right now? Is there something that is happening in your life today where you would like to see better results, a better outcome? If so, the first step is to notice what it is that you want to change.

For example, you want to start walking a bit faster than you have made your habit, and you notice that each time that you are not focused on walking faster, you go right back to your old pace. Then, you can shift your focus back on swinging your hands a little bit faster and a little bit higher. While you are still changing this to make it permanent change, it is important to notice each time you revert to your old walking pace and then, start to swing your hands faster and higher. You need to do this until your subconscious mind realizes that this is your new walking style. Then, you will no longer automatically revert to your old walking pace. You have created a new recurring event in your life — a new lifestyle — you have changed your reality.

YOU ARE FREAKING AMAZING!

It's so amazing that you can change whatever you want to change in your reality, simply by giving it all your attention until the change is permanent.

Do you want to get a higher salary, a better job, or start your own business? When you do something for the first time, you need to look at what others have done who have achieved the same results you want to accomplish. For example, do you know someone who has founded a company before? If so, you can go to that person and learn from them. You need to look at and learn from those who have already achieved the success you want. You have a much better chance to achieve whatever you know others have done already.

The human body is incredible. Your body is incredible.

Here is one example of how incredible the human body is. Before the year 1954, several scientists had made statements about the fact that the human body could not run a mile under four minutes. They said, it simply wasn't possible, that the human body is simply not created to be able to run the mile under four minutes. In May 1954, Roger Bannister ran a mile in under four minutes. Do you see how remarkable it is that when he broke the record, two other runners ran the mile under four minutes, only two months later? This is one example of many that shows us that when you know that someone else has done what you want to accomplish, it is much easier for you to achieve the same results in anything you want to achieve.

YOU CAN ACHIEVE ANYTHING YOU DREAM ABOUT. YOU ARE INCREDIBLY POWERFUL!

When you do things over and over again, you get better and better at what you repeat over and over again, just like you get better at reading. What you are going to notice when you become good at something is that people start noticing your progress. You might even hear someone say to you, "You're so lucky."

This is a very common attitude people have who look at you today with your current results or your new talents. They totally forget about all the work you have put into achieving this new talent or results. You are so good at finding recipes online or meeting new people who bring you opportunities that others do not get, or you always get hired at jobs others fail to get. This is because you have made the right decisions, taken the right actions, and thought the right thoughts that have enabled you to be in the right place at the right time and be able see when opportunities are being presented to you. This is all about the exercise, doing thing over and over again!

That is how you create your own luck! You will always get luckier and luckier the more you practice. The more I practice, the luckier I get. So, the real question is whether it's really luck or not. If you look at the ability to be in the right place at the right time and say the right things to get an opportunity presented to you, as luck, you know that you will always get luckier and luckier the more you practice.

You are lucky!

You are so lucky to be here right now.

You are lucky to be you!

No one else is so lucky to be you.

ONLY YOU ARE SO LUCKY AS TO GET TO EXPERIENCE HOW GREAT YOU ARE!

The next time you spot someone you think is lucky, be sure to visualize more than just the event you are observing right then and there. What has that person done in preparation to become so lucky? What has that person gone through to be there, to be that person, to be so lucky? Almost without exception, the person who succeeds at something has made a lot of effort to get there.

When you see an iceberg, you're only seeing about 10 percent of the iceberg, because there is about 90 percent of the iceberg underneath the surface. When your friends see you reading again and again and see how much your reality is shifting for you, they might think that this was easy for you. But, no matter how great you feel and how easy this seems to you now, you've done a lot to be able to experience this as being easy. You have taken the initiative, and you have been taking action again and again.

You are the creator of your reality.

Now, take your hands and spread them apart, as though you're going to give someone the biggest hug you've ever given. Your hands should be in a straight line, from your shoulders, pointing in opposite directions.

Take both hands and place them on your opposite shoulder, wrapping them around you. Give yourself a huge hug — you deserve it, because you are freaking great.

Do that now!

If, by chance, you have not been doing any of the exercises so far in this book and we are now at the end of chapter three, this book is very unlikely to have a huge impact on your life. If it feels awkward to celebrate yourself or give yourself a hug, find a place where no one can see you. I promise you that this book will be 25 times more powerful and life-changing if you go ahead and get over whatever might have been stopping you from doing the exercises. Most likely, you are right here, right now smiling and doing everything as you read through and enjoy it, because that is what you decided to see for yourself when you started reading this book — to see if you are really as freaking awesome as I know you are.

Now, use the time to experience yourself in this present moment. Feel how awesome you are right now!

Feel how unique you are.

YOU ARE UNIQUE.

Enjoy experiencing yourself in this present moment and enjoy being you right here and right now!

04

OUTSTANDING

YOU ARE OUTSTANDING TODAY!

You are on your fourth chapter now, and that, by itself, is outstanding. It was your decision to take the initiative to get this book, and it was you that took the action needed to start reading it. It was you that executed the plan; well done. It feels great to know that it is all you, because you already knew you could, and you did. Now, you have even further confirmation of how freaking awesome you are.

Great job so far.

You should be very proud of yourself right now, because you are amazing. You are implementing your plan, and you are taking action daily. Many people who start a new venture quit too soon, before they reap the rewards, but you are different: you will not quit. If you have already fallen off the horse on your way to this chapter, we can safely assume that you picked up where you left off, or you would not be reading this right now. That is something all of us can learn from you.

We can all learn how to start again. When we fail, we can pick up where we left off and continue with our plans and reaching our goals. By doing that, there is no failing, just taking a break. That's exactly what you do.

CONGRATULATIONS ON THAT ATTITUDE; IT'S AMAZING!

Did you know, that time, as you perceive it, is an illusion. There is no past nor future, only the present moment, right now. Your consciousness is expanding, and this expansion is pushing you to make a change, to grow and develop on your soul's journey. It is not wise to hold back this process with procrastination. You know deep down what changes you need to make in your life right now.

Worry and stress! Worrying what if this or that happens will only lead you to more suffering and feelings of paralysis. Your mind will continue to take you in circles. When you feel pressure, relieve the pressure by taking action. Do not delay taking action. Practice this today and for the next few days. Take action on what you have not done in your past moments. That thing that keeps popping up in your mind over and over again, but you did not take any action on before. Something just came to your mind right now, say it out loud, recognize it, own it, and recognize that it is something that does matter in your heart, and that you want to do this. Then, do it.

You are a human being. You are your mind, body, and soul. They are your vehicle. A practical system you need to take care of. Your vehicle receives information and nutrition, processes it, and then, produces results. Your vehicle needs great care if you want it to perform at the highest level. The balance of your vehicle influences your abilities to perform. It dictates what you can accomplish and what you can experience. For example, if you overeat, it will greatly impact your ability to perform.

BALANCE IS THE KEY.

You can try to overeat. Stuff yourself for a few days in a row, and see how it affects you. Then, compare it to when you eat only what you need with great love and respect towards your food and yourself.

One-time overeating makes a big difference. When you eat too much, you can feel it right away, and sometimes, you can even feel it the next day, almost like you have a hangover. Your body will feel heavy, slow, sluggish, and sore. Everything has an effect on your well-being and abilities.

You are awesome; you were given this life. This life is to live to your fullest potential. Every single day, you are given the opportunity to start this day again, a fresh start. It is up to you to use this opportunity well and be grateful for getting one more day. Gratitude for life and the things life has to offer is one of the keys to your happiness.

Now, list everything you can think of that you can be grateful for right now. Say it out loud. You do not have to scream it, just say it, so you can hear it yourself. There is nothing wrong with having a conversation with yourself. Remind yourself of all the things you can be grateful for. Say out loud, "I'm grateful for..." and then, what that is.

This exercise is great to help you realize how much you truly have to be grateful for. Everyone has experienced something they need to work out, something or someone they have lost, or something they have a problem with. It is yours, to work out these problems in your reality, the problems you chose to see in your reality and face them and start seeing the good in life. Your perspective is what creates problems. With a simple decision, you can easily change a problem into a challenge. Identify all the love that is all around you trying to help you have the most pleasant life possible. Be grateful, and start to enjoy what life has to offer. Now, count out the things you are grateful for right now.

Take one minute to do this now!

Life is a roller coaster. There are many things you have already endured. All kinds of emotions, all kinds of events, and all kinds of happenings. Yes, all kinds, and it needs to be celebrated, because it means you're alive. You have this life, and you get to experience what life gives and what life takes. Everything your mind can create or experience has its opposite: hot, cold, down, up, bad, good, right, wrong. In your reality, you get to experience both. To know what cold is, you need to experience what hot is, otherwise, you do not know the difference between them or what it is like to experience it. Life is a work of art, and you are the artist of your own artwork. This is the art of living!

Now, lift your hands directly above your head, and keep them as straight as you can, pointing them to the sky. Take a deep breath in. Hold your breath for five seconds, and if you can, stretch your hands even higher. Then, release the air out with power. At the same time, let your hands fall down by your side. Just be careful not to swing your hands into something when you do this; it might be best to stand while doing this.

Do this three times.

Now, you feel better!

Are you here in the now, or is your mind taking you somewhere else? One of the things that makes you human is your mind. It is important for you to expand your mind and expand your horizons, so your understanding, tolerance, and patience are not limited. So that you can see things from many angles, not just one.

All obstacles are just another challenge. You can solve them all, with time and love. Activate your mind in a beautiful way, so you can start to see the unseen and understand the consequences of each action you take, so you can live a happy life.

You are what you think; remember that. When you give your mind space to experience a broadened horizon, you open your mind and get to see things from different angles. You stop looking at things through a tube, and your understanding will grow, and the experience will be powerful. You can put yourself in their shoes and others get to be as they are, without being judged by you, because you know them, and you can feel them. You have empathy.

We are all one; we are all connected. You understand that in this world, everything is energy. Energy is in motion all around you, and everything you see is energy in one form or another. The food we eat, our clothes, everything. When you allow yourself to grasp this idea, your mind becomes wide open, and you will start to see and experience this more and more.

One big smile towards a stranger is energy exchange. You're always exchanging energy. Practice this energy exchange with the people around you.

Money is energy. When you pay for goods or services, you exchange energy. Whoever created this product that you are buying is giving you energy in the form of goods, something you wanted in your reality, and you give him your money in exchange: another form of energy.

Everything is energy — everything!

We are always exchanging energy.

You are pure energy!

What do you see?

How do you feel?

Can you smell anything?

How are you breathing?

Are you smiling?

Are you happy?

YOU ARE FREAKING AMAZING!

You are fantastic, and the world feels you right now. You are you, and you are freaking awesome!

Say this with your inner voice right now. Read it twice:

> *I love life.*
> *I love life.*
> *I love what life has to offer.*
> *I'm going to enjoy all the good things in my reality today!*

So that you may change something in your life, you must accept yourself exactly as you are. Love yourself 100 percent, and forgive yourself 100 percent. Take the steps you want to take with love towards yourself. You may say something inappropriate or do something without thinking about the consequences, but that is not what matters here. What matters is that you are going to forgive yourself. You will not break yourself down for any ill-considered thoughts, for they are not yours, unless you focus on them. Just let them pass through.

You still have a lot to learn!

I just wanted to let you know that what you have been doing by reading this book is absolutely amazing; you have been putting yourself in first place. When you put yourself in first place, you have the energy needed to serve others as well. You have been preventing yourself from running out of gas by putting yourself number one and not putting others before you. By doing that, you have really been treating yourself with respect. You will not run out of fuel, because you have been taking initiative again and again.

YOU ARE TOTALLY AWESOME.

Remember that although you have been unleashing the creative power within, you are still human, and your vehicle needs you to take good care of it. Let's pretend you are a car. Think about which car is the nicest of them all, and you are it.

If you are out of gas, does it matter which car you are? You are absolutely amazing. You have been preventing that, so you don't run your batteries dry. You have been rapid-charging your batteries while reading how freaking awesome you are. Your batteries are fully charged right now, and they are ready for your next move. In the unlikely event that you do not believe me, I am going to give you a task to prove it. Go wherever people you know personally are. Go directly after reading this chapter, and give them a hug. See how much you can give, now that your batteries are fully charged. See the effects you will have on them, now that you have put yourself number one.

If no one is at home or close by, go ahead and hug the next person you meet. Just remember to smile first and ask:

Can I give you a hug? I am just so energetic right now, and I want to share it?

You are so amazing to be investing in yourself by reading this book. Everyone who knows you will notice that you are putting yourself number one and feeding your vehicle with positivity and the praise you deserve.

YOU ARE FANTASTIC.

Feel all the creativity that you have unleashed within you right now.

YOU ARE UNSTOPPABLE.

You deserve this. If anyone deserves it, it's you. Congrats on being number one.

I want to thank you from the bottom of my heart for reading this book. You are the reason why I wrote this book. You created me. Your need was brought to me through the collective consciousness. I listened, and now, this book is in your hands.

YOU ARE AWESOME.

Now, go home and hug the person who came to mind earlier. Go now, and hug someone with all this creative energy that has been unleashed within you.

05

BOB

YOU ARE UNSTOPPABLE.

You take each day and tackle it like a champion.

How do you feel today?

Have you asked yourself that question today? If you do not feel great right now, don't worry. Just wait a little bit, because you're going to feel fantastic in a short while.

You're going to feel great, because you can simply decide to feel great, and then, it happens. As soon as you decide to feel great, you start to feel better right away. That's how amazing you are.

Do you focus daily on carefully selecting what you say to others? Many people are constantly watching what they say to others and always try to speak in the best possible way, but often they forget to filter their words in the same way when they speak to themselves.

How do you speak to yourself when a thought pops into your mind? Have you talked down to yourself and convinced yourself that you cannot do something or that you don't feel like doing it? This is very common; most of the time, you are going to be your worst critic.

At some point in your life, you have probably heard someone say, "You just have to believe in yourself, and then, you can do anything." Maybe you've heard, "You must believe that you can do it, so you actually can do it." This is often not the absolute truth. Did you know that often people who succeed in something that they did not have faith in themselves in the beginning?

How can you start your journey, when you do not believe in yourself in the beginning?

Now, I am going to tell you the secret that many people have used to become great at something or ridiculously wealthy, or managed to do something that was so absurd in mind in the beginning that when they reached their goals, they had the rub their eyes and pinch themselves a little, just in case they were dreaming. There are many people today who reach all their goals, no matter the magnitude of their goals. For those people who are experiencing their dreams, it sometimes becomes hard to tell if their life is real or if they are simply living in a dream. That is because those people are experiencing their dreams daily.

Are you getting curious to know how you can start your journey without believing in yourself? If you are, I understand. This is a well-kept secret, and that is why there are so few people who achieve remarkable success in life. It is so hard to take that first step, because how do we get the faith needed in ourselves to start?

The secret is empathy.

Empathy is when you can put yourself in other people's shoes and see things from their perspective. When you can understand what that person is going through and feel what that person is feeling. You may have experienced this when someone close to you lost a loved one and you experienced their loss, with your empathy. You may have experienced it when your friend finally finished something that was a big deal in their life, such as graduation or finishing a project that took a long time to complete. You experienced your friend's happiness, and you became sincerely happy for your friend. We all have this ability to experience through our empathy, but, of course, it varies how strong we can experience it.

The secret that people who want to do something big with life but do not have faith in themselves to start the journey use is to use their empathy and experience the faith other people have in them. Yes, you are right; this does not sound complex at all, and this will be very easy for you to do, because you are freaking awesome. If there is anything you would like to achieve now, but lack the faith in yourself to get started. Simply go and find someone who has faith in you. Someone who believes in you. If possible, find someone who has achieved the success you want to achieve, or at least someone who is more successful than you are right now. The reason is that those who have already achieved great success know and believe you can do it as well. At some point, they were standing where you are today. A successful person will almost never discourage you. For example, a person who has founded a company will never say to you, "This will be impossible for you to achieve." Instead, they are more likely say something like, "Yes, of course you can. It's much easier to found a company than I thought it would be when I started my first company. You simply do A, B, C, and you are all set."

You can use your empathy and experience their faith in you to get you going long enough until you start to have faith in yourself.

Does this sound too easy?

If so, then it's great news. You already know that this will be easy for you. For example, have you been wanting to write a book, but making it a big deal in your mind to the point that the task has now become a monster? If so, go and find someone who has published a book, and talk to them. Tell them that you want to publish a book, and all of a sudden, you have killed all the excuses you have been so good at creating up to this point. All the excuses you have created simply do not make sense anymore.

I do not have any spare time to write a book.

I cannot write.

My grammar isn't good.

I work too much.

I am afraid.

I do not want any of my friends reading the book.

These could be some of the excuses a person would create to sell themselves on the idea of avoiding doing something new. There is one question that matters the most when taking the first step. A question to ask yourself right now.

Why do you want to do it?

Why do you want to do the thing you have in mind? If the reason is something other than money or just because, you have a good enough reason to start right away, right now, today.

I want more time with my family.

I want more time with my kids.

I want to travel more.

I want to work less.

I want to change the world.

I want to leave some kind of legacy here on earth.

I want to experience more.

I want to grow.

These are all great and valid reasons why you should start right now, today, after reading this chapter. Step one: find someone who believes in you, and use your empathy to start your success story right now. I know you can do it. Deep inside, you know it as well.

If you are scared to approach someone to help you get started, here is something amazing. Start by writing one page today about why you wrote the book, as if you have already published the book. Imagine you have already completed the book, and write a short one-page chapter called *Why I Wrote This Book*.

This small thing might be all you need to get started.

Another fantastic idea is to make your book really short. Make it ten times shorter than you imagined it has to be, and then, publish it yourself. That small book is enough to open the floodgates. You can use services like lulu.com to publish the book and print it, without any help. You could also publish it as an eBook on Amazon. It is that simple. Yes, you can do this in a very short time period, because you are freaking awesome.

Fear of something new is a very natural thing to experience. It is a very human emotion. We all have a Bob inside of us. It is a metaphor of the events that occur when you create excuses why you cannot do something.

Bob has stayed with mankind for millions of years. He was placed inside us at the very start of our existence. He was put there so we would not walk off a cliff or walk straight into the mouth of a saber-tooth tiger, or, for that matter, to prevent us from trying new foods or dare outside the safe cave we hide in. Bob screams inside of your head when you step outside the box you have created around yourself. He screams, "You are going to die!"

This box is also known as the comfort zone. When you try something for the first time, you become afraid. That is Bob, who does not know what's next, the unknown. Try to do something new, and he will automatically assume that you might actually die. He is very convincing in your mind.

Now, visualize this little guy in the head who jumps up and down when you are going outside the comfort zone, screaming, "Don't do it; you are going to die."

This might happen, for example, when you are about to present your first lecture in front of a crowd. You know it will not kill you, but, somehow, Bob manages to make you feel like you will actually die. If you have this metaphor in mind, you might even see the humor in the situation. Imagine this little guy, Bob, jumping around, screaming in your head.

Bob is very exaggerated, and if you take time to stop and think about this metaphor when you are about to do something new, you will have an easier time putting Bob in the back seat of your vehicle and telling him to keep his mouth shut.

Now, I am going to share another little secret with you. Have you noticed that when some people who succeed in something — in other words, when they reach exactly the results that they intended to reach — something happens? Let's say that they set themselves a goal to workout and lose 20 pounds, and after a certain time, they manage to reach this goal, but soon after reaching their goal, they gain back all the weight they lost.

This is called self-sabotaging your results.

Have you seen this happen before, or have you experienced this yourself? This is common, but those who succeed and then maintain their success know this little secret I am going to share with you right now.

Do you want to know what the secret is? Are you a bit excited to learn what it is? I hope so.

The secret is that those who maintain their success have already set another goal, a second goal. When you reach your first goal — for example to lose those 20 pounds — you have reached the end of the road. The end of the planet, the end of the world, so to speak, if the planet was flat. This is when Bob takes control, because he does not know what's next. You and he are now standing on the edge of the unknown. He will then start to sell you the idea that you must get away from the ledge; it's too dangerous here. Go back to the known, go back to your safe zone, go back into your safe cave.

You and Bob know that there is no danger in your comfort zone, no threats, nothing new, and nothing unknown. If you want to keep your 20 pounds off permanently and not self-sabotage your results, you need another goal behind the first goal. You always need to have two steps in front of you. In this example, it could be to lose two pounds in the next twelve months, after you reach the first goal. Or maybe your second goal might be to change your diet, perhaps to change one meal per week into something super-healthy to keep your current results. Do you see where I'm going with this?

Now, Bob knows that you are not on the edge of the unknown. You still have another step, another goal to achieve. But you must always have two steps in front of you and that means, that when you reach the first goal, you must set another goal behind the second goal, always two steps in front of you. Your third goal might be to add another meal each week, and change it into something super-healthy for the next six months after that. It really does not matter what the next goal is that you create to have that second step in front of you. What matters is to not let Bob in the front seat of your vehicle. Bob tends to grab the steering wheel, and he could easily make you self-sabotage your vehicle. I can't stress this enough: Bob is a terrible driver.

KEEP BOB IN THE BACK SEAT WITH TWO STEPS IN FRONT OF YOU ALL THE TIME.

You are made of pure energy, like everything else in this world. All you see in your reality is energy. This is scientifically proven, and you do not need to understand it or even believe this more than you have to believe in the law of gravity. This is how it is. You are energy, whether you believe it or not. Energy cannot be destroyed, nor created. It is only possible to transform energy into another form of energy. Change fat into muscles, water into vapor or ice, and so on.

If we would ask a scientist to explain to a child what energy is, it might sound something like this:

Energy has always been there, and it will always be there; it cannot be destroyed, nor can it be created.

If we would ask a priest to explain what God is to a child, it might sound something like this:

God has always been there, and he will always exist. He cannot be created nor destroyed.

Is it possible they are talking about the same thing?

Energy is always in motion. Energy is never still, and so are you; you are always in motion. If you are not growing and prospering, you are, essentially, slowly dying. You are growing right now while reading this and being motivated mentally and physically. You are growing right now.

When you solve a puzzle or play chess or do anything that strains the brain, you are also growing. You should try to find something new to learn every day. Just like you're doing right now, you are growing and prospering right now.

You are pure energy.

YOU'RE FREAKING AWESOME.

You and all the actions you take are what makes life so enjoyable. You are a creator. Once you have read this book and practiced what you have read, when you have mastered the content and understood every single thing and implemented it in your life, then, you have to pick something else. Something new to learn, yes, you must keep growing throughout your life, because if you are not growing then you are — you know the answer, right? I can say this to you now, because you have reached this level, this far in the book, which means that you have great willpower and such massive energy inside of you right now and you understand this. It will be wonderful for you to continue to learn and grow with each passing day, for the rest of your life.

YOU ARE FREAKING AMAZING!

Next time you are walking around other people in public, take your hands and swing them in a circle. First, the right hand. Swing it in a whole big circle. Then, the left hand. That is a very simple exercise for you to step outside your comfort zone. Just a small step outside your comfort zone, but enough to feel how easy it is for you to accomplish that. Remember to visualize Bob comically if this task seems too hard to achieve. You will not die; this small action will only make you stronger.

YOU ARE IN CONTROL.

Now, take a few seconds and just enjoy being yourself.

Feel how awesome and in control you are, right here and right now.

06

THE FUTURE NOW

> *You know what? You're really getting the hang of this. You are consistent, and you keep coming back to read more. Ready to experience yourself again and again, simply by being you.*

YOU ARE SO FREAKING AMAZING TODAY.

Yes, amazing. I know I cannot see you right now, and I do not need to see you to know that you are amazing, because I know what's inside you. We all have the same core. We are all connected.

I KNOW YOU CAN DO ANYTHING.

We all have a part inside of us that knows no limits; you were born that way. Unfortunately, today's society begins to limit you at an early age. You have been fed with all kinds of nonsense about what you can and cannot do all your life.

You have been limited.

You have been told how to stand, how you should behave, how to think, how you should wear makeup, how you should wear your clothes, sit, chew, speak, and how you should be in general! No wonder that most of us, today, think we cannot do something.

It has been imprinted from childhood by our parents, teachers, advertising, radio, interviews, television, friends, and the world wide web. Your abilities to create your own reality is so strong that you have managed to create a limited reality. First, you decided to listen to this bullshit that you are limited. Then, eventually, you started to believe it, and that's when you manifested your limited reality.

I have good news for you today. Since you have this tremendous creative power to limit yourself, you also have the creative power to unlimit your reality. Keep in mind that you have been creating this limited reality for many, many years now, so to change it back will take longer than just this one chapter. The good news is that when you start thinking in a positive way, removing those limitations you have created for yourself, you can do it in an incredibly short amount of time.

Very soon, you will be able to go and do something you do not believe you can right now.

You can simply make a decision now, while reading this chapter, in this moment, that you want to live your life without limitations.

I say that, because you are the only one who can stop you from limiting yourself.

Let's take a few examples of something you might have possibly been letting stop you, until now.

I do not have the time, but I would really like to do this.

Start to ask yourself and write down for one week everything you do. How much TV do you watch? How much time do you spend on Facebook? What are you spending your time on that you could replace with doing something you truly want to manifest in your reality? You might be shocked when you see how much of your time is spent on *not* creating what you truly want in your life. You might become light-headed when you see how much time you really spend on simply letting life pass you by, doing things that make you less than you truly are. You can always find time to do what you truly want, if you want it bad enough. No matter how successful a person is, we all only have 24 hours in a day.

I never have the money to do what I want to do.

Have you looked at how other people who did not have the money did what you want to do? Have you looked at possibilities to create extra income? Have you done what many consider the hardest thing to do: have you written down everything you spend your money on? Write down everything — I mean *everything* — and see how much you can actually save. Maybe that is the best way for you, but that's for you to decide. Excuses or solutions?

I am too heavy to do this thing that I want to do.

Check if there is any person in the world who is heavier than you, who has accomplished what you want to accomplish. When you find that someone who has done it and that person is heavier than you, then what excuse will you try to use next? You could also choose to lose some weight, if that is how you feel about it. You could start slowly by strengthening yourself and losing weight by simply walking outside on a regular basis, and you would most likely lose more weight than you think right now, because by reading constructive positive materials, like you are doing right now, you are working on your mindset, which is your strongest weapon in creating and manifesting whatever you desire.

Do you believe that anyone who changes their mindset can decide to have a faster metabolism or lose more weight, for example? Do you spend some time each day visualizing yourself as you want to be? If not, why not?

You should be very grateful right now for being you, because you are doing an outstanding job so far.

You are putting yourself number one.

You are actively transforming your life into what you want it to be like in the future, but it's happening right now.

It is often said that there is a thin line between love and hate. Did you know that it is also a thin line between being grateful in the now and using gratitude as an excuse not to grow? Gratitude is a powerful weapon when you use it the right way.

> *Gratitude is not something you should use to become comfortable in your comfort zone. It is not something to become stagnant and stop your growth. Gratitude is something that you use to help you grow and prosper.*

Now, think of three things you are especially thankful for today. If you cannot think of anything, just allow yourself to feel gratitude for being alive, for being able to breathe, or for waking up this morning. I know that you have something you are thankful for, something you cherish dearly. Now, say it out loud. It is up to you how loud you want to say it, because the volume does not matter, only that you say it. Are you ready?

I am so thankful for....

Nice work, and again:

I am so grateful that....

Very good, and now, one more:

I am so grateful....

Those things that you just listed out loud are things you should think about more often.

> **When you experience gratitude, your energy vibration becomes exceptionally strong and powerful.**

Once you are ready and you have decided to bring something new that you want into your life, you can raise your energy vibration with gratitude, and that will help you attract and manifest things, relationships, and opportunities that support your manifestation into your reality. The process of manifesting something new into your life is done by writing down anything you want to happen.

You write a date in the future on a piece of paper. Let's say three weeks and one day ahead into the future for this example, and you are writing about the previous day in past tense. You could write down something like this:

I'm so grateful that I accomplished this. I was able to read one chapter each day this month, not missing a day, and I can feel the difference. It is a staggering difference in this short amount of time. Now, I am glowing each day, and I can't help but to smile when I look into the mirror. When I woke up yesterday morning and stepped on the cold bathroom floor tiles, I felt the life force awakening within me as the chill from the floor traveled up through my body. It felt refreshing and blissful. I looked into the mirror while smelling the faint perfume smell still lingering from last night in the bathroom. I heard the birds singing my favorite song outside the bathroom window. I smiled at the person in the mirror, and the person smiled back. I truly felt how beautiful and amazing this person is, and I began to smile even more, and so did the person smiling back at me in the mirror. I almost started to giggle, because this felt so strange. It felt so strange to think back only three weeks ago when the person in the mirror looked very different from today. Now, today, it is impossible for me to see anything other than this beautiful and amazing person I see in the mirror. I am beautiful and freaking amazing! I did it! I celebrated it by treating myself to a massage at the new massage parlor downtown last night. What a day!

This example I just described to you, is called stepping into the future now, and it's also called writing a future diary. You can do this daily with anything you wish to manifest into your reality.

The key to manifest what you write in your future diary is to describe the future event as they have already happened in the past tense. Describe your feelings at that moment in past tense and in as many details as possible. Experience those feeling as you write them down. The more gratitude you can feel for the events you describe, as though they are already accomplished in your future now, the faster you will manifest them into your reality. The more details, the better and more accurate it will manifest. Describe how the texture of things were in the future which has already come true. How are people talking about your success? Describe how strangers are coming up to you to compliment you on this victory, on this goal you just achieved. Describe who you are thanking for your success and so on. Try to use as many of your senses in your description as you possibly can. Your touch, voice, smell, what you hear, what you see, and what you feel. The more you experience the detailed description in your future diary, the more powerful your manifestation becomes.

What will you write down today that you want to manifest into your reality? Don't be afraid to try this. What is the worst that can happen? That nothing changes, that's the worst-case scenario, but what is the best-case scenario?

Think about it!

Each day from now on, for the next 30 days, write down something that has already happened in your future. Something you have already accomplished in your future. Something you want to manifest into your reality. Write down how you feel now that it's already true.

The biggest step is simply deciding that this will happen. Your mind will immediately begin to notice things you need to notice for this reality to become true. You will notice new things in your reality, because you will have shifted your focus with that decision.

Which means you have already changed your reality just by deciding it.

Remember that your subconscious mind does not know the difference between what you dream of and what you experience in your waking hours, even when you are daydreaming. As long as you allow yourself to experience the feelings that are associated with achieving this specific goal that you have already accomplished and experience it through as many of your senses as possible, you will manifest it. To make this process even more effective, take out time — as often as you possibly can — to remember, to recall the event that has already happened in your future. In the same way you recall memories from your past present moments, do the same for your future events that have already happened, that have already been manifested in your reality.

YOU ARE SO INCREDIBLY AMAZING.

You are much more powerful than you can imagine right now. Your thoughts and actions in the past are the reason why you are exactly here, right now, reading this chapter, reading this book. You could not have changed a single thing in your past without changing the fact that you are here right now reading these words on this page. If you did, you would be somewhere else, doing something else.

> *You can take full responsibility for your life today. You know it's all thanks to you and it's all your fault, too — no one else.*

You are the creator. You have created your reality as it is today, and now, you can change it again, if you want to.

You might have questions like, *If I take full responsibility for my life now, how is it my fault if someone runs into me on a bike? Isn't it the other person's fault?*

The answer is NO, absolutely not. Not in your reality. It is in his or her reality, but not yours. You own 100 percent of your reality, no one else. What you did and thought created the perfect opportunity for you to be exactly there at that specific moment, to be able to get hit. If you woke up sooner or later that morning, or if you would have walked faster or slower, you would not have created this perfect timing and perfect placement to be able to get hit. You did everything perfect for this could come true — you created this opportunity, you are the creator or your reality. If you do not take responsibility for something in your reality, you have given away your creative power. You could not change anything in your reality, if it is someone else who controls and is responsible for your reality. If you have been a victim of thinking someone else is responsible for your reality in the past, this the perfect day to reclaim your divine creative power and start taking the controls back in your reality. Only you are responsible for your reality.

What would you like to create in your future right now that has already come true?

You are your own creator. You create your own reality each and every day. Whether you do it on purpose or not, your divine creative power is very powerful. So why not start doing it consciously from now on?

Now, take one hand and stretch it as far up into the air as you can and hold it like that for five seconds, and then, switch to the other hand and stretch it up into the air, as far as you can, like you are trying to touch a star in the sky. Hold that pose for five seconds as well.

Do this now!

Great, now move your hands in a manner that you have never done before. Choose whatever move comes to your mind. Make crazy non-logical hand movements. When you are done, put up a huge smile.

Do that now!

By doing something you have not done before, you have altered your perception of your own reality. You just changed your reality. Although this was only a small change for you, it showed you how fun and powerful you are. You probably looked like you were having loads of fun, if someone would have seen what you just did.

YOU'RE TOTALLY AWESOME.

You totally stepped outside your comfort zone.

You are so alive!

Now, use a few seconds to think about what you are going to write down in your future diary today? What are you going to describe, and how powerfully are you going to allow yourself to experience the great feelings that come with achieving this goal or task you have in mind? Use the time to think about how great you are right now and how much you can change your reality with a single decision, thought, or action.

Experience yourself and enjoy how wonderful you are, right here and right now.

07

THE DREAM CAME TRUE

> *You are back at it.*
> *You are doing great things by taking action again and again.*

You are freaking awesome.

In this chapter, you are going to think about the way you talk to others and how you talk to yourself. First, I want to tell you this: if you don't already know it, words have a strong and lasting effect on your environment, yourself, and others, even on the food you eat. How much impact can words really have?

When you carefully select your words and say something nice to others and to yourself, you positively influence their energy vibration. You influenced and therefore, increased their energy levels and your own at the same time. Now, focus all your attention on this story I am about to tell you, and try to experience this story as your own. Put yourself in the shoes of the person in the story.

You are a child, and you just said something that was highly inappropriate, but you just don't understand that your words have this great power. You think you can simply say anything without it having any long-term effects, but, thankfully, your parents hear you speak. They start to explain to you that you are changing the environment in a bad way when you talk like that. You are very surprised, and you don't really understand what they are trying to tell you. Those are just words, for crying out loud. What harm can they really have? You parents see that you don't understand, so they set a mandatory task for you. You must hammer a nail into the old tree in your backyard every time you say something bad, and your parents will help you to know when you are impacting your environment or others in a bad way from now on.

Now, you are learning, but this is not going so well for you. You have nailed a new nail into the tree every day for 30 days in a row now. As a child, you start to think about the workload. You do not feel like having to hammer a nail into the tree every day, so you start to become more selective of the words you use, more mindful. You are tired of having to hammer a nail into that tree all the time. It's not that you understand yet how much impact your words are having; you are only thinking about ways to stop having to hammer that damn nail every day.

You start to say beautiful things and praise others. Your parents notice this positive shift in you and tell you that from now on, each day that you use beautiful words and have a positive impact on your environment and others, you can pull one nail from the tree. You are on a roll now. It's been another 30 days, and the final nail is coming out today. The nails are all gone. Well done, you did it, and now, you are standing in the backyard looking at the wounds in the old tree. What can I do to mend this? How can I fix the holes?

You cannot fix the holes, any more than you can take back the words you have spoken that had a negative impact on your environment or people. Your words leave sores for years, but they will eventually heal. It just takes a long time.

Have you ever spoken and had this metaphor in mind before you select your words?

Do you realize that by putting someone down or talking in a negative way towards others that the damage can be long-lasting? Don't worry; this story was just meant to wake you up a bit. The good news is that you can prevent any long-lasting negative effects from now on by thinking twice before you say something negative towards others again and for that matter, towards yourself.

Words are powerful. You are powerful.

The next time you see something that irritates you at home, use this one question before you react to the situation. I will use a simple example to explain this to you.

Let's say that your husband, boyfriend, girlfriend, roommate, or child is always leaving the kitchen cabinets open, and it annoys you like crazy. In the past, you have complained and nagged about it. You just don't understand why they can't just close them, like you have so elegantly been nagging and getting upset about.

The next time this happens, ask yourself this question:

Does this have any effect on what I want out of life?

My goals?

Does this have any effects on the things I want to experience in life?

Does this affect what I want to create?

Does leaving the cabinets open have any effect on me reaching my goals or not?

I think it is highly unlikely that it will, but, on the other hand, it can have a long-lasting negative impact on your goals to verbally abuse the situation or nag about it. You could end up throwing your future train off the tracks and even breaking the tracks, which have been laid out towards your dreams.

You create negative energy by irritating yourself on this matter. If this does not affect what you want in life, it's time to drop it. It does not matter when you look at the bigger picture. This does not matter at all.

Now, go and find yourself a dictionary if you have one in your home, and if you don't own a dictionary, write this word on a piece of paper.

The word is, **problem**.

If you own a dictionary, take a pair of scissors and cut this word out of the book. No matter how expensive the book was, this is a symbolic ritual for you to start moving faster towards your goals and learn to apply your energy in a positive way. Next, throw this word in the trash, bury it, or burn it. **Problem** is a word that you are no longer going to use. Instead, you are going to adapt a new word.

The new words are **opportunity** and **challenge**.

Choose which one you like better.

What you considered as a problem before, you will now refer to as a challenge or an opportunity. If you have no dictionary at home, write the word **problem** on a piece paper and throw it in the trash, bury it, or burn it. I know you are starting to realize how powerful a small ceremony like this will have on your subconscious mind. I know you know this will make a big difference in your life. It will change many things in your future by never again using the word problem. Now, you only speak of challenges or opportunities.

Let's try it out, right now!

Let's jump back to the same example with cabinets. Now, you will rethink what caused you to become irritated before and look at it as an opportunity. You could say something like this to yourself:

Wow, this is great. Now, I can finally get new hinges on the cabinets, so they will automatically close by themselves.

Wow, I am always getting new opportunities. Wow, I'm lucky.

If you plan on using the excuse that the new hinges are too expensive, you are creating a new....

What was that word again?

I know you must have already forgot it, so let's just use the new word: then you are creating a new opportunity.

You could solve the challenge by putting several rubber bands together and tie them in all the cabinets, so that the doors will snap shut once you let go of the cabinet doors, and because they will actually slam shut, make sure to put some pads on the doors, so they do not chip or break.

Well done!

This is just a very simple example of how you can solve your new opportunities and challenges that present themselves to you, in your daily life.

Does this challenge make any difference in whether you will achieve your goals or not?

If not, it is not worth getting upset about. Instead, you will proceed directly to solving the challenge or grabbing the opportunity.

I KNOW YOU HAVE BIG DREAMS!

Are you actively working towards your dreams on a daily basis, or are you actively creating excuses to do nothing about it?

Do you think you might regret trying to make your dreams come true?

Do you think there might be a slight possibility that when you are about to leave this life, here on earth, that you will say:

The thing I regret the most in my life is that I followed all my dreams?

Do you hear how crazy that sounds?

Why are you here?

Why were you born?

It's so simple. You were born in this world to experience and learn!

You are here to experience, and there is no right or wrong when it comes to experiencing — it's all an experience. When you decided to be born here, it was because you wanted to experience what you're experiencing right now for your soul journey.

But now, possibly, just maybe, you want to start experiencing something different. Perhaps, you have had enough of what you have been experiencing in life. Maybe you have learned your lessons and want to start experiencing something new, something better. Maybe you want to start making your dreams come true. Maybe your experiences have served you the spiritual growth you needed to start this new chapter. You can rest assured that if you pursue your dreams, you will be happier and more fulfilled. You will be happier the whole way there, not just at the finish line, when you have finally manifested your dreams. New dreams will be born on your journey, so if you are lucky, there is no finish line, only a lifetime of wonderful challenges and victories.

You are very quick to adapt when you get something new in your life, like a new car, new house, new pool, or a new adventure. It will not be exciting for a lifetime — you will always need more or something new to achieve because of your super-adaptability.

YOU WANT TO GROW YOUR WHOLE LIFE.

Some choose to live their life in sadness. For those who do, the sadness is never at the same level, because you become accustomed to it, like everything else in life.

YOU ARE SO FREAKING AWESOME AT ADAPTING.

If you choose sadness and become accustomed to it, your creative power will kick in to create even more, so you can experience more of it. If you select a happy life to live, you will get used to it as well, and then, your creative power kicks in again and starts to create more, so you can experience more.

> *The universe will always deliver more of what you are experiencing now. Your vibration tells the universe what you want more of.*

It's time you give yourself permission to manifest your dreams. Time to give yourself permission to be happy. If you haven't already made that decision — to be as you were intended to be, as you were designed to be, by Mother Nature and not society — go ahead and decide right now. Go ahead!

Now, let's look at the five things people say they regret the most in their lives right before they pass away, and let's see if you can improve any of these five things in your life right now. Nurse Bonnie Ware, who worked at a hospital in Australia, asked each patient on their deathbed, with less than two weeks left to live, what they regretted the most in their lives. Here is the list:

1. I wish I would have tried to make my dreams come true, instead of living for others.
2. I wish I had worked less.
3. I wish I had the guts to share my feelings more and say what was on my mind.
4. I wish I had kept more in touch with all my friends.
5. I wish I had allowed myself to be happier.

Is there anything on this list that you can improve today and not have to regret later?

Can you call someone today who you have not contacted for a long time and just say, "What's up?"

Or, even better, can you go to that person who came to mind and knock on their door and say hi today?

Do you have someone in your life who you have neglected to keep in touch with?

It does not matter whether you're in top physical shape or incredibly wealthy, poor or in a bad physical shape. It does not matter whether you have achieved great success or little success at anything. Forget about all that right now, because that does not matter in regard to this task of keeping in touch with friends and family.

Is there someone who you want get back in touch with today?

Do you want to make your dreams come true?

What dream came to mind? Say it in your mind or, even better, say it out loud — that always works better.

How do you feel now that you realize that you are the only one who can stop you when it comes to manifesting your dreams?

I bet you feel good about it, but maybe you got a knot in your stomach, as you might have realized that you could have already achieved some of your dreams or started to work towards them a long time ago. No worries, it does not matter whether you are 20 years old or 70; you can start right now after this chapter.

Do you want to work less?

Why?

What feelings can you experience while thinking about not having to work so much?

Are you happy?

Do you want more happiness?

You'll be glad to hear that you can easily become happier!

You are adorable. I wish I could see your face right now.

Are you smiling?

SMILE!

Smile, and raise the energy levels in your environment right now.

SMILE!

Wow, now that is what I call great energy exchange! Thank you for smiling!

THANK YOU FOR BEING FREAKING AWESOME!

Are you ready?

Who has been stopping you?

I know the answer, but do you?

Now, take your hands and clap them together in front of you, and smile for 10 seconds.

Do that now!

Hooray! This is you applauding the awakening that you are experiencing.

This is you applauding how great you are right now.

You are applauding the fact that you can do anything.

You have no limits!

I am so happy for you right now!

You can do this.

You did it.

You feel great!

Now, take some time to think about all the things you are going to start doing today, and when you finish this chapter, go and drink a glass of water, and say to the glass:

Who drinks this water will be healthier, who drinks this water will heal the body, and who drinks this water will become happier. Thank you, I love you!

Yes, that is right, you say I love you to the water. It's all about the vibration you are formatting the water with, about the vibration you are creating in the water. You are much more powerful than you know.

You deserve it, your body deserves it, you are amazing!

Remember and experience how truly great you are right here and right now!

08

SUPERSTAR

> *Wow, another chapter. You are on fire!*
>
> *Your decisiveness and strong will is exceptional, something others can look up to and follow.*

YOU ARE POWERFUL AND DETERMINED!

You know that you want to read and learn more, therefore, you take the initiative and execute your will by starting another chapter. You are not governed by the will of others. You live your life for you, on your terms.

CONGRATULATIONS ON BEING SUCH AN AMAZING HUMAN BEING!

There are many ways to manifest what you want in life. There are many ways to make your dreams come true. One of the best methods is to write down on a piece of paper what you want to manifest into your reality. What matters most when you're writing things, people, opportunities, or experiences into your reality is to write them down in as much details as possible. Experience it and write it as though it has already been done, in the past tense. Write how it feels when it has already come true.

You are essentially tricking your subconscious mind to believe it's already true, by experiencing all the feelings that come with achieving that goal. You did it! By experiencing it now, your current vibration tells the universe what you want more of, and that is what you manifest into your reality.

There are plenty of other methods that also work well to manifest things into your reality.

You can tell someone, with passion and feelings, what you intend to accomplish. One of many ways it could manifest is when you tell people what you are planning on accomplishing and you say it with passion and emotion behind the words. Then, it is not unlikely that someone who hears you speak about these plans and with passion, will be the person who will make it possible to manifest this dream of yours into your reality. Maybe someone who hears you speak knows a person who can help you, or knows someone who is looking for a business partner, or the best thing that might happen is that the person listening will be the one to help you achieve it.

It's important to remember this fact: those who have already achieved success in life remember when they were taking their first steps and the help they received along the way to be able to achieve their success. These people are often more than willing to do the same, to pay forward what was done for them in the beginning. One day, it will be up to you to pay it forward, once you have manifested your success story.

Giving back is truly a big part of long-term success. The sooner you start to give, the sooner you will start to receive. I hope you understand that I am not talking about giving with the attitude of receiving, not giving and expecting something in return, because that is not actually giving.

When is the best time to start giving to charity or to help someone in need?

YOU SHOULD START GIVING RIGHT AWAY, TODAY.

Like with so many things in life, you should start before you are ready.

There is an incredible power that comes from giving.

Perhaps, you feel like you have nothing to give right now?

Maybe you have sold yourself the idea that you cannot give anything right now?

There is nothing abnormal about that idea. When we lack or need, we tend to hold back on giving, but let me share a little known secret with you right now.

May I inform you?

If you cannot give ten cents out of every dollar you make today, you will not be able to give 10 million out of 100 million in the future. That is because it's always going to come down to your attitude towards life. When you give, you get.

> *You can rest assured that everyone who has achieved great success agree that they did not achieve real success until they started unselflessly giving.*

Maybe you are like many others right now who have created their reality based on the lack of. Just maybe, you experience your life as a deficiency. If you have a mindset of deficiency right now, as you keep growing, so will that mindset of lack. Therefore, it is very unlikely that you will reach your desired success with such a mindset. The good news is that since you had to power to create your reality based on the feeling of lack, you can decide right now, while reading this chapter, to dedicate yourself as a person with the mentality of abundance. If you do that, you will have shortened the time it takes to succeed and increase your chances many times over.

One of the most important steps to take in the process of achieving success or in the process of starting to receive something you want into your reality is to envision the person you will become once you have achieved your success.

Will you be generous then?

Will you start giving once you become successful or achieve your goals?

Will you be able to give then?

Will you be able help those in need then?

If so, then you must become that person right now, today! That's the moment when life starts to happen for you! That's when you will be presented with opportunities and people who will help you on your path.

YOU MUST BECOME THE PERSON YOU SEE IN YOUR FUTURE, RIGHT NOW!

That's when you start to see results on your path. Yes, I know, it works in reverse. Once again, first you visualize your goal in the future. The next step is to see and experience what type of person you will become then. The third step in starting your journey to success is to remember and become that person, right now, today.

What other methods can you use to get what you want out of life now?

You can take a few minutes every night before you fall asleep, with your eyes closed and visualize for yourself, what you are doing when you have reached these goals.

How do you feel?

Who are you?

Who are you talking to and thanking for your success?

How do you feel now, when you visualize everything you can possibly visualize about your future self, with your eyes closed?

What emotions do you experience?

How many detailed emotions can you experience and visualize?

When you visualize this with your eyes closed, how much of your future self can you feel and experience?

I know that you are so powerful when applying yourself to experiencing this that you might have to visualize this some time before you go to bed at night. Your creativity is so powerful that you will most definitely get your heart racing a little faster, and you will feel so empowered and energetic once you start visualizing all your future successes as a daily routine.

You are the real deal!

You are a lean, mean creative machine.

YOU ARE FREAKING AMAZING!

What else can you do to accelerate your process in manifesting your dream reality?

You can talk aloud to the universe!

Some people talk to God, but it does not matter whether you are religious or not, you can always talk to the universe; it is always listening. The energy that is out there — the universe — is listening to the vibrational frequency you are sending out right now. It is your energy vibration that communicates your wants to the universe or the source. The universal consciousness receives your message and delivers it to whomever needs to hear it or feel it. To those who are aligned to your energy vibration and can help you make this reality come true. In other words, the universal consciousness plants ideas and seeds in the minds of those who want to do something that is in alignment with your dreams. Believe me, there are plenty of people with aligned purposes in this world.

There is always someone who is looking for what you are thinking about and what you want to accomplish. There is always someone thinking about something that is in alignment with you and your thoughts.

It only takes one person, one chance, one opportunity, or one deal to change your dreams into reality. To experience and live the dream as you visualize it.

What else can you do to make your dreams come true?

You can role-play with someone you trust. Someone who is willing to help you evoke the feelings associated with already achieving your goals. This can be a very fun exercise to do.

Do you want to try it?

I am going to allow myself to assume that you are nodding your head right now, eager to role-play. Yes, I love that attitude, well done!

In this exercise, we will say that your dream is to become famous, just to use something to illustrate the point of this exercise. You know that children do this all the time when they play doctor, cops and robbers, or mommy role-playing games, and so on. They are really good at it, and so were you once, too. Now, it's time for you to invite your inner child to come out and play again.

You are the person who walks into a room and everyone knows you, but you do not necessarily know anyone in the room. You are extremely successful in your profession or in your field — whatever it is that you have in mind right now.

Come on now, just play along. If you need privacy, I suggest closing the book right now and moving into a room where you can participate out loud. If you're unable to participate out loud, do it with you inner voice and remember to experience it with strong emotions.

What is that thing that you have become so very successful at?

Think about what that is right now.

What is it that thing you want to do or want to be better at?

Do you have it in mind yet?

Great, because now you have become a celebrity, thanks to your exceptional success, and you have become so wealthy that you can travel anywhere in the world, anytime, and yes, of course, all first-class. No, wait, better yet: you have your own jet to travel wherever you want to go and whenever.

Now take a look around you, where you are right now!

Do this now! We have started role-playing!

Look, there is someone coming to you right now, just stay calm. It's probably one of your fans.

Amanda, your number one fan:

Hi, wow, I can't believe it. It's really you. I saw you from over there and just had to come over and say hi. I hope I'm not disturbing you too much. I see you're reading a great book right now. I have read it also, and I loved it, almost as much as I love your work, and that says a lot about this book. Do you mind, can I just tell you that you are my biggest role model today? Your sheer willpower is so incredible. You are such an inspiration to many, especially me. You inspire me daily, and I have been becoming a better person each day because of you.

I have been waiting so long, to finally meet you face to face. I played this conversation in my mind, over and over again, and now, I just don't know what to say, really. This is so surreal to be here right now in front of you: my role-model, my inspiration. I really look up to you.

May I ask you a question?

You may now say, yes.

Yes, it's okay, so say it, inside your head or out loud — it doesn't really matter; you are role-playing!

Amanda, your number one fan:

Can I just ask where does all that energy you have come from? To be able to achieve such great success like you have?

Now, create an answer in your mind.

Where do you find all that energy?

Answer this now!

Great answer!

Now, experience it in your mind, how it feels to be this successful. Doesn't it feel great?

You are a role model for so many people right now.

Amanda, your number one fan:

Wow, I did not expect that answer. I knew you were incredible, but wow. Now, I am really starstruck. I know you are incredibly busy changing the world for the better and reading this fantastic uplifting and fun book, but I would really like to ask you one more question, if that's okay?

Go ahead. You know the drill by now: say yes!

Amanda, your number one fan:

Whom or what do you thank for achieving this massive success you have achieved?

Create an answer!

Whom or what can you thank for you massive, massive, massive success?

Whom are you thanking?

This book? (just kidding)

Your personal trainer?

Your family?

Your coworkers?

Your coaches?

Your children?

Your teachers?

Your spouse?

Your banker? (another joke)

Think of whom you would like to thank for having achieved this incredible success in your life, and remember modesty for your own abilities and your ego is good when you are thanking someone else for your success. Give credit where credit is due. Your gratitude for the things, opportunities, and people who help you on your way, is what is going to help you achieve this massive success and sustain it.

Go ahead and answer this now!

This was one of many ways. You can use to manifest what you want to become true in your reality. You see that in regards to most things you do, there is not just one right way to do things. There are many ways to achieve your goals.

Have you heard of the movie *The Secret*? I am referring to the movie, because I did not read the book myself. What was the movie missing? They had the mindset, energy vibration, and thought processes in there, but what was missing? They forgot to tell you to take massive action at the same time. Some people watched *The Secret*, went straight home, sat down, and tried to manifest their dreams without taking any further action. I loved watching *The Secret*, no disrespect here!

Achieving your goals and sustaining them is roughly a three-phase process.

> Phase One
> is 100 percent action. You must make a decision, pick up this book, hire that coach, or take some kind of action to start the whole process.
>
> Phase Two
> is 80 percent mindset and 20 percent what you take action on, to achieve that success.
>
> Phase Three
> is when it balances out. To sustain the success you have achieved, you must apply 50 percent mindset and 50 percent action.

This means that if you plan to achieve more than you are achieving today, but you plan on taking action without working on your mindset first, it is very likely that you will have a very long and hard road ahead of you on your journey to success. All action and no mindset change, is a journey we sometimes refer to as the rat race. If you plan on achieving success without working on your mindset first, it will be like a hamster on a hamster wheel. Have you ever seen a hamster wheel? Does it matter how efficiently or fast the hamster runs on the wheel?

Will he ever get anywhere?

The same can be said about your success story, if you plan on only using your muscles instead of using your whole vehicle: your mind, body, and soul.

I know you would not plan to use excessive force and simply grind on. You know better than that.

You can be extremely proud right now, you have reached this far in the book and you now know more about how to create and shape your reality than about 70 to 90 percent of humanity. You now have so many methods and tools to achieve whatever you would like to achieve in the shortest amount of time.

Now, you are going to perform a little experiment. You are going test the power of your mind right now.

Raise one of your hands straight out in front of you and hold it there.

Now, imagine that I am placing a three-pound bag on your wrist. Visualize this now! Use your creativity and tighten up your hand a little as I place the bag on your hand. You feel it right now. You feel the weight all the way to your shoulder, and your hand becomes heavier. Visualize this as powerfully as you possibly can. Release that creative power you have from within. Your hand keeps getting heavier and heavier. You know this is imaginary, but your mind is so powerful that you can feel the pressure on your wrist and the weight on your shoulder. With your intention, let your hand start dropping down very slowly because of the weight. You are doing a great job. I know it's heavy, and I know you can do this.

Yes, you are doing this, getting it done.

You still feel the extra weight on your hand, and now, I'm going to lift the bag off your arm. It's gone!

You feel the weight is off. Release the tension in the arm and feel how much lighter your hand is right now and feel it start to rise again. Just let it rise to its original position, then, drop your hand all the way back down into a comfortable position again.

Wow! You did an incredible job just then, and I hope you are smiling right now, because you are amazing!

SMILE!

You are amazing, and you feel incredible.

Congratulations!

YOU ARE A SUPERSTAR!

If you did not feel any of what you just read, you can simply practice this again until you get it. Anyone can unleash the creative power within. Some people need more practice than others, but I suspect you got it on your first try.

Now, use some time to think about the person you will become once you have managed to become wildly successful, whatever your success looks like. Use some time to figure out what you need to change today to become that person right now. Be the person you envision right now. Be the person who has already achieved all your wildest dreams right now, today.

YOU ARE SUPER FREAKING AWESOME.

Feel yourself in the present moment and feel how completely confident you are, that you are already a superstar, right here and right now.

09

GOOD NEWS

Welcome back!

What's up?

What I mean is, what's new?

Yeah, what's new out there?

I do not mean, just with you, but in the world?

Do you follow the news?

Do you know how terrible the world is?

Have you read it or heard it somewhere?

If you follow the news in general, you know exactly what I am referring to when I ask if you know how terrible the world is. Reporters are experts in negativity, but it's not their fault; it is the masses that demand more negative news by talking about them and by giving them the most attention. You see, as a reporter, you are always looking for ways to create the news that is the most read or most talked about.

When we look at statistics, it's clear that negative gossip or news is the most read and gets the most attention by readers. So, when they are selecting which news should be placed in the newspaper or on the television, they will more often select negative reports, rather than the positive ones.

But, of course we see some good news, as well, but they do not get as much coverage. They do not get people to gossip and spread the news as effectively. You feel much better when you are being positive and surround yourself with positive people. As a matter of fact, you feel incredibly fantastic when you live your life in a positive way, by surrounding yourself with positivity. You have been taking action, like reading this book, getting positivity and fresh new ideas to implement in your life. Reading constructive and positive material which you soak up and it becomes a part of you, and you feel absolutely fantastic in this positive environment.

But, what do you do when you put the book down?

Do you go and turn on the news or read about something terrible?

If you do, you feel how your energy vibration shifts immediately. You want to live a positive life, because it so freaking amazing.

> **You cannot expect to live a positive life and yet continue to surround yourself with negativity!**

You don't think that will work, do you?

You can choose, for example, what you see on your Facebook news feed. If you see something negative that makes you feel bad from some of your friends online, you can choose to unfollow them. You do not need to see a negative news feed on your Facebook feed or any other social media for that matter. You do not necessarily need to unfriend your negative friends on Facebook or other social media, but you can select to unfollow the negativity. It is not helping you to transform your life into the life of your dreams!

Do not read anything that makes you feel bad on your social news feeds!

Do not read anything that drains you!

Instead, read something that gives you energy, something positive, like this book or one of the many others that are filled with positivity.

IT'S YOUR CHOICE!

Some people have chosen to live a negative life, and they often find that by reading something that is more negative than their own lives, they somehow feel better about their own misery. Those who have decided to live a negative life are not like you. Unlike you, they do not realize that you can choose to live a positive life, simply by starting with the decision to live your life in a positive way. First you decide, and then, you start to bring positive things into your reality.

Many of the most successful mindset coaches or life coaches in the world will start by telling their clients to stop watching the news, because they know that if you're going to succeed in anything, it all starts with positivity and a positive outlook on life. From now on, please stop letting the media program you. You have done that long enough, haven't you?

One way to accomplish living a positive life is to avoid negativity, at least in the beginning, while you are taking your first steps in the shift to living a positive life.

There is a rule of thumb that states that if you look at the five people you spend the most time with, you are the average of those five people. This is not always the case, but it is very likely true most of the time. For example, if you become very depressed, you will start to associate yourself with a new crowd or even no one. If you start to live an extremely positive life and achieve great success, you will also start associating yourself with a new crowd. You start attracting more positive and successful people into your reality.

> ***You are always either growing and prospering, or slowly shrinking and dying.***

The same applies to companies; they are either growing or dying. In this world where everything is made of energy, nothing stays still. You never stay at status quo.

If you would like to take your personal development and put it into another gear and step on the accelerator on your journey to success, you need to think very carefully about who you want to have around you.

Do you want to have people who have done less in life than you around you?

Do you want to be the smartest person in the room? If so, you are choosing to not grow, and therefore, you are, essentially, slowly dying. If you want to continue to grow and thrive, you need to surround yourself with people who motivate your growth. People who know more than you and have done more than you or people who have done what you intend to accomplish. By doing that, you will grow the most, and your energy vibration will be at a level of energy that supports your journey.

To keep on learning and growing, you need to choose good books to read or listen to. You have been making good choices like the choice to start reading this book.

YOU HAVE BEEN DOING A GREAT JOB SO FAR.

It's absolutely awesome that you have chosen to grow and prosper, and what you will soon see — if you haven't seen it already — is that you will start to attract people into your reality that support your growth. You are radiant, and the positive energy you possess shines from within, and people with the same mentality are attracted to it.

> *Please remember this, though: some people will not feel comfortable around you when you are at your best, and that's okay.*

They are not aligned to your energy vibration. Their vibration is much lower, and they will not be drawn to you. They might even be repelled by you.

One of the best references you can use to know if you're really starting to grow is when people start criticizing you. When people begin to say things like:

You should not be doing all this work.

It's time to relax.

You have gone too far.

You must enjoy life and stop trying so hard.

You should stop now; it's never going to work out anyway.

When you start to get criticized, when you start to see the haters appearing in your life, you know that you are really making great progress in your growth. When you become more than before and when you are growing, followers will come to you in many forms. One type of follower is your critics, your haters. It is good to know that right now, because once the first critic appears in your reality, you can use your positive attitude and celebrate it!

> *When your first hater arrives, you know you are on the right track.*

If, at some point in your journey, you start feeling sad or negative, grab it by the balls, and kill it right there, while it's still only a seed.

Don't plant it in your garden!

The simplest way for you to get out of the state of sadness or hopelessness is to go and do something nice for someone else, make someone else happy and cheer them up.

Do you believe this or not?

Try it next time you feel a negative feeling creeping in. Swallow your pride, and go make someone else happy. Then, share with someone else how you overcame your negativity that had started to creep in, by bringing joy to others. Do you see the pattern here? You make someone else happy, and in exchange, you receive positive energy in return. When you take this energy with you and share with someone else, you are creating a spiral of positivity.

IT IS BETTER TO GIVE THAN TO RECEIVE.

This spiral is often referred to as a vicious cycle. In modern society, a vicious cycle is mostly understood as something negative, but you can change that, and you can start looking at a vicious cycle as the most positive thing ever.

A vicious cycle of happiness!

A vicious cycle of joy!

A vicious cycle of fame!

A vicious cycle of progress!

A vicious cycle of love!

You might have heard the saying, the rich become richer and the poor becoming poorer? This saying is 50 percent positive, right? The more you surround yourself with happy, successful, loving people, the more you will experience exactly that in your own reality as well.

YOU WILL CREATE A VICIOUS CYCLE OF GROWTH.

A fun way of looking at these positive vicious cycles is to look at them like an amusement park ride. You show up to this positive amusement park every day, and you stand in the middle of the park and look around you. Then, you say to yourself, *Which ride should I try today? Maybe I should try the vicious cycle of happiness today, or maybe I should finally ride the biggest ride in the park: the vicious cycle of personal growth. Yes, I think I will do that one today.*

This amusement park is freaking awesome!

**YOU SO GOT THIS RIGHT NOW,
AND THE UNIVERSE FEELS YOU.**

Right now, you are moving so much positive energy all around you.

YOU ARE SIMPLY AMAZING.

Do you have something in your home right now that has a positive effect on you each time you look at it?

Do you have something on any of your walls that tells you how great you are?

Do you have something you see every day that reminds you to smile?

> *The task for you after this chapter is to find something you can place in your home that will trigger a positive attitude or make you smile.*

Search for something you associate with love, happiness, or positivity, and put it somewhere you can see it at least twice a day. The bathroom mirror, closet door, by the front door, or somewhere you will see as often as possible. This will often make your day, by simply reminding you to be the best version of yourself.

I am also going to give you another task, right now. When you are about to go to sleep tonight, set up six alarms for tomorrow. Take out your phone right now, and create six new alarms on your phone for tomorrow.

Eight a.m., ten a.m., twelve noon, two p.m., four p.m., and six p.m.

Do this now!

Now, you are all set for tomorrow. When these alarms go off, take a 15-second break from whatever you are doing to smile, whether you feel like smiling or not. You may also close your eyes and experience the feeling of love, happiness, or anything positive that comes to mind for those 15 seconds. If you prefer, you may also use these 15 seconds to close your eyes and experience what it feels like to have accomplished the goal that keeps popping into your mind. Embrace the moment, and take these 15 seconds to shift your energy into a higher frequency, and see how the day will play out in a better and more positive way.

Remember to find something to place in your home today that reminds you of how great you are or reminds you to smile.

There is nothing automatic about being happy; it's always your choice. Yes, even when you encounter something in your reality that you might think is out of your control, a shock of some sort. We all encounter setbacks in life. What makes you happy in life is not what happens to you in your life, but how you deal with it.

> *Happiness can be the subtle difference between whether you react or respond to events and emotions.*

Have you ever seen a person who gets stuck in a wheelchair after an accident, but is still truly happy?

That person was very likely happy before the accident. When a person who has chosen to live a happy life all the sudden loses their legs for whatever reason, they will soon find a way to deal with that and become happy again. After adapting to their new reality, that person becomes a happy person in a wheelchair.

A sad person who loses their legs will become a depressed person in a wheelchair. You understand this. You know deep down that this is all a decision you must make. This is all up to you. Of course, you may seek help to be able to live a happy life, once you decide you are going to live a happy life. You might have decided already that you want to live a happy life, but you are not quite sure how to change your current situation. Getting help works, and it's a sign of strength, whether you are reading this book, listening to audios, listening to your coaches, friends, or family. But before you can get help, you need to decide you are going to be happy, because otherwise, you will not listen to the advice or processes presented to you. You need to want to be happy. Maybe you are already a happy and positive person today, because you decided to be one a long time ago. If so, ignore what I just said. You are probably shaking your head, thinking to yourself, *Why don't others just decide to be happy like me? Why don't people decide to be happy and put up a smile like I do?*

No matter which side you stand on today — happy or unhappy — you can always add more and give more of yourself. You can help others do the same by sharing your happiness, by sharing the ways and habits you use to sustain happiness.

Do you think happiness or love is something that's kept inside of a box with limited space?

It is not uncommon for new parents to feel this way, because their love for the first born is so great they can't imagine that there is any room for more. They love their child unconditionally. Then, when they become pregnant again, a thought sneaks in, for a brief moment, *What if the box is already full? How can we love the next child as much?* Then, when the second child is born, like magic, the box expands itself to double the size.

> **This is how it works with feelings and love: there are no boundaries or limitations.**

If you are bursting with love and happiness right now, you can always add more to it.

YOU ARE UNLIMITED WHEN IT COMES TO LOVE.

This happens with ease when you are in the vicious cycle of love. The more love you give, the more love you receive. You get happier and happier, and you become more and more thankful.

What are you willing to remove from your house today? What is currently in your home that makes you feel bad or sad when you look at it? Perhaps you have a statue that triggers a knot in your stomach when you see it, but you don't want to get rid of it, because it is an heirloom. If you do have something sitting around you home that brings you sorrow, sadness, or in any other way lowers your energy vibration, just by looking at it or being around it, you have already decided you don't want to be happy. Yes, you did, by purposely having something around that makes you the opposite of happy. It's your decision, your reality, your life. If you have decided to be happy, but still have something around you that makes you unhappy, you need to stop this nonsense right now! Throw it away, give it away, or at least box it up and smile while you are doing it. You will feel how the energy shifts in your home by doing that.

GET RID OF THE THINGS THAT MAKE YOU FEEL UNHAPPY.

Do you have any doubt? Do you think the Chinese philosophy Feng Shui is just a made up nonsense? Is there a possibility that you do not believe you must have good energy in your home to feel better? No, you would never believe that, because otherwise, you would not be reading this chapter right now. You know that the flow of positive energy is very important on your path to happiness.

You are doing great.

YOU ARE GREAT!

It's so amazing how you take everything you learn in this book and you take action. You own it. You make your life more wonderful and joyful every day. You are the reason why this book was written in the first place. Written for positive people like you.

CONGRATULATIONS ON BEING SUCH AN AWESOME HUMAN BEING!

Now, take one of your index fingers and point it at yourself right now. Point it anywhere on your body. It does not matter where, just make sure it's pointing at you.

Do that now!

Yes, exactly like that.

THIS IS YOU SAYING, "I MATTERED."

You are the only one who can experience what you are experiencing right now.

You are unique.

You did it.

It's okay to be proud right now. You are absolutely fantastic, and it's time for you to know that, if you do not know that already.

Now, think about what you're going to make visible in your home, in your life, that makes you happy and what you're going to remove that affects you in a negative way. Enjoy taking 15 seconds out tomorrow to raise your energy vibration and seeing how wonderful the day will be. Enjoy feeling the awesomeness that is residing within you, right here and right now.

10

LISTEN

> *Another chapter — you are outstanding!*
> *There is no question about it: you are doing a fantastic job!*

You keep taking the initiative, and you read and read some more. It feels so good to look forward to the time you sit down and continue to read. Lately, you have been looking forward to your reading time, and you feel great right before you start.

When you do something you have done before, it doesn't mean you will have the same experience again. You have, for example, been reading new chapters in the same book for a while now, yet you've had new experiences each time.

It's amazing how it works, because you have been doing exactly the same thing with different experiences.

Have you ever read a book, watched a movie, taken a course, or learned something that completely changed your reality?

It is very likely that, at some point, you've experienced something so great that the experience totally shifted your reality. After you experienced a change in your reality, and you do exactly the same thing later in life, like reading the same book. In your new reality, do you think it is possible to experience a shift in your reality again, the second time reading the same book?

It is possible, especially if you have been reading books that help you look inside and assess yourself. Books that help you assess the situation today. Books that help you look at where you are and where you want to go. Books that help you see how you can keep growing, developing, or changing something you currently do that's not serving you. If you are reading those kinds of books, it is very likely that you can experience something completely different when you read the book again later. This also applies to films, seminars, and audio recordings. The reason you are experiencing something new when you listen again is that you have grown into your new current reality. You have experienced something new, something different than you had experienced the first time around. Your reality, your knowledge, and your understanding is completely different the second time you read the book. The second time around, you notice something new that you did not notice the first time or something you did not understand. You interpret the same information in a different way because of where you are now, and because of your new skillsets in life.

Let's take a simple example to explain this even better. You read a book about new parents and how new parents face the world and what feelings are associated with being a parent. When you read this book the first time around, you were not a parent yourself yet, and you interpreted the whole book based on your relationship with your mother. The next time you read the book, five years later, you are a proud parent of three-year-old twins. When you read it the second time around, you interpret all the information in the book based on your relationship with your twins. The experience of the book becomes so different that it might as well have been an English book the first time and a Chinese book the second time around. The experience will be so different that it is unbelievable that it is actually the same book. You understand the content differently now, when you read the book again, and now, you can implement things from the book into your reality.

The same thing happens to you on a daily basis with things you might take a little notice of today, but, when you start to learn more about them and gather knowledge, you suddenly start to see something completely different. Let's create another example.

You have a plant in your home, and you look after it, but it's just a plant, for now anyway. On your birthday, you are given a book about plants, and in the book, you learn all kinds of interesting things about plants that you think are fascinating, like the fact that if you talk to the plant every day, it grows faster. At first, you find this hard to believe, but, since you are such an open-minded person, you decide to challenge the idea and try it yourself. You might just be trying to disprove those statements. Regardless of your true intentions, you try it out for yourself. Three months later, you are in shock when you see that the plant has grown as much as it did in the previous twelve months before you started talking to the plant. Yet, you have a hard time believing what you are witnessing with your own eyes. You see that there is something going on with the plant; it is clearly thriving. Now, your reality has shifted. You become more interested in the plant and seek even more information to read about plants.

You find a book that is about how plants grow, how they reproduce, how energy affects them, and some life hacks to help the plant become even more beautiful. Eventually, you become obsessed with your plant. You start looking forward to waking up early each morning, getting your cup of coffee, and taking a look at your plant. You have started to grow feelings for the plant. It's yours, and it's a really nice plant. Almost every day, you notice something new about the plant. One day, you decide to start looking at your plant with a magnifying glass, and you see that she is all covered with small needles that look like hair. The hair needles are so small that you need to bring out the old microscope you have stashed away in your closed, to take a better look at them. The hairs on the plant are soft, and you notice that when you play music, they react. You see that it's almost like the plant begins to dance when you play music. Now, you start to experiment with different kinds of music and soon find out that classical piano music has the greatest impact on the plant. Your reality at this point is so much different than from the day you were given the book about plants for your birthday. You can never see the plant again with the same eyes you did in the beginning. At first, you only saw a plant and now, you see this complete ecosystem, which you now call by name — it's your Amanda.

The same is happening to you right now, today, while you're reading this book. Every time you learn something that could be considered simple, but you did not know before, it changes how you see the world, sometimes small changes, and sometimes enough to totally shift your reality.

Are you smiling now?

SMILE!

Why did you smile?

Was it because you know what it does for you, or is there another reason why you are smiling?

Are you happier?

If you are not, you have not yet decided to be happier, and that is the most important part of the process to become happier. The decision to become happier.

Do you believe that you are the architect of your own reality?

If you believe that, it is very likely that you have already decided to become happier, but if you find it hard to believe, and perhaps, you experience yourself as the victim in life, I have a good idea for you to try. Contest what you're reading here — go ahead, just try it — decide to be happier, smile more and think about beautiful things. Think beautiful thoughts, just so you can prove to yourself that this is all just bullshit in this book. Perhaps you do not dare — what if this is all true, and you would accidentally become happier, and you would start to smile more?

Would that be so bad?

I think you know what's going on here. We are playing mind games, and that is why I spoke to you the way I just did. You can create the reality you wish. You can create the reality you strive to experience, no matter what that reality looks like to you. You can create anything you want. You just need to truly desire it and follow the process of attracting it into your reality. It's easy to get stuck and think this life is out of your control. Many people stay there their whole life.

If you have been waiting for a while now, for the right methods and mindset to change, I must ask you, are you ready now? I am talking about *right now* at this very moment as you are reading this sentence. Are you ready to change your reality into what you have been dreaming about?

ARE YOU READY TO TRANSFORM THIS DREAM OF YOURS INTO A PLAN AND EXECUTE IT?

Say it out loud and with conviction. You owe yourself that much.

Do you need a bigger reason or better reason to change, or are you already well on your way to creating the reality you want to experience?

There is something that keeps drawing you back to this book, to the next chapter to learn more. There is a desire within you that drives you on. There is something that makes you hungry to know more.

Have you identified what it is?

Do you know what you want?

Do you know what you want to experience?

Each time you make a decision and start acting on it, your life become more and more interesting, and you start to see more and more of all the beauty your life has to offer.

Now, put your attention on the top of your head. Put your hand there if you need to, just make sure your attentions is completely there.

Now, think about the big dream you have decided is probably a little bit out of your reach. What is this dream that you have decided to believe you cannot achieve?

The dream you keep telling yourself that you will not be able to achieve because of the lack of time, lack of money, or something else that you do not have to be able to achieve it.

WHAT IS THIS BIG DREAM OF YOURS?

Think only about that dream right now and say it out loud, or inside your head, if you prefer to repress it further — your choice. Recognizing that this dream is there is so liberating. Admit that this dream is still alive inside of you. It's still there.

Say it out loud now!

Awesome job; you did well there.

Awesome to see how you are beginning to dare to do and say more and more. It suits you well.

Now, turn your attention to a small dream you have, which you know you can totally reach, but you have not accomplished this dream yet, for whatever reason. You have a small dream inside of you that you know as soon as you start to act on it, it will come true.

WHAT IS THIS LITTLE DREAM OF YOURS?

Is it to go and see lions on a safari?

Is it to visit London?

Maybe it is to visit your grandchild abroad?

Buy a new car?

Finish knitting that sweater you have not found the time for yet?

Getting a dog, but you have not yet been actively looking for one?

What is this little dream you have, which you know you can fulfill so easily by deciding to execute it?

Say it out loud now!

Brilliant, you are on a roll now.

Now, use your creative power within and start experiencing what this small dream will feel like, once you accomplish it. How does it feel to have this little puppy licking your face and celebrating your arrival home after a hard day at work? How does it feel now, sitting in your new leather recliner in the living room that you have finally finished refurbishing?

How does it feel that you have finally gone through all the boxes in the garage, thrown all the garbage away, and are finally painting in your garage, like you have been planning to do for so long?

> ***How does it feel now that you have grabbed this dream by the throat and said, "It's time for you to come true," followed up by taking action, taking control, and deciding to put it on your front line of priorities in life?***

Are you smiling? I hope you are.

SMILE!

There you are!

Do you know why I asked you to think about the big dream first?

John's dad runs a herring fish factory, and one day, John needed some herring barrels, so he went to his dad and asked him for 100 herring barrels. His dad almost lost his temper, but when he calmed himself down, he asked John if he had gone mentally ill. John responded very calmly and asked again, but this time for only 50 barrels. His dad did not like that question any better and asked if John was joking. John did the same as before, asking for fewer and fewer barrels each time. Finally, John said, "Okay, I get it, can I at least have one barrel?" His father said, "Okay, that's no problem."

What John knew is that his father would have never agreed to give him this one barrel that he got, if he would had asked for it right away. John only needed one barrel for his project.

Hint! Hint! Wink! Wink!

In the same way, you thought about the big dream first, making the small dreams seem so obtainable now. It's going to be so easy for you to finally take action and start fulfilling these smaller dreams first, leading to you starting to believe that you can achieve the big one!

Perhaps, the big dream that came to your mind is something that you have to learn, something new to learn.

Do you want to do something completely new and exciting, but when you have dared to think about it, you have gotten a knot in your stomach for years now?

Is the big dream to experience something or to create something, but you are afraid you will fail?

Are you afraid to fail? Has Bob convinced you that you are probably going to fall over the edge of the unknown if you try to accomplish that dream?

If you are afraid to fail, and no matter what you have tried, you just can't get over the fear, then I have an alternative method to get over that fear. Use your fear, use Bob to accomplish this big dream. If you cannot put Bob in the backseat of your vehicle and start taking action on your dream, feed Bob a bigger fear to protect you from!

Be more afraid of what will happen if you do not change anything in your life right now!

Be more afraid of regretting not trying. If you cannot put Bob in the backseat of your vehicle, make Bob gigantic and start fearing to stay where you are and slowly shrinking up and dying!

Be more afraid of not trying, and if you are about to fail, be more afraid to get stuck not trying, than you are of failing!

Be more afraid not gaining the experience of failure and moving one step closer towards your big dream, than of failure itself.

If you cannot take Bob and place him in the backseat of your vehicle, make him bigger! Use him to start growing and performing because of your fear of not trying and regretting it later.

Be more fearful of not growing than ever failing.

This only applies to you if you haven't been able to overcome your fear of failure. Take the method that works best for you and use it to take the first step you need to take, to get started today, right now.

**GIVE YOURSELF PERMISSION TO LIVE
THE LIFE OF YOUR DREAMS.**

Make your dreams come true — you deserve it and you know it in your heart.

You will be very unlikely to succeed in the first attempt, but it could happen. You can increase your chances significantly by getting a mentor or a coach to help you achieve the dream. If you do not succeed right away, some people might call it failure, but you know better. It's only one step closer to the goal.

REMEMBER, IT IS NOT POSSIBLE TO FAIL UNLESS YOU STOP.

What some people have decided to call failure, you call an opportunity to learn to do things better or experience what you should not do. It's all an experience and a big step forward towards your dream, however bad it might seem as it is happening.

The opportunity to experience not reaching the goal in the first attempt is what helps your soul grow the most. Start failing as soon as you can and as often as you can, because, then, you are taking steps towards your dreams. You can easily accomplish your smaller dream. Make up your mind right now! Make a decision. Are you going to start tonight or tomorrow morning? Just choose right now! You have spent enough time thinking about this little dream. Now, it's time for you to grab this dream firmly and make it happen.

> *Feel all this positive energy that you have today. You cannot fail. It is all just steps that move you forward that must be taken and experienced to manifest this dream.*

Now, you have my permission to start feeling excited about this dream you are about to manifest into your reality!

Are you getting pretty excited to get going and write it all down on a piece of paper to start your journey?

Can you call someone you know who can advise you or help get you started?

I know I am super-excited on your behalf, just like my coaches were for me, when I started to make my first little dream come true.

You are incredibly amazing, a force to be recognized.

You can do it!

You can do anything you decide to accomplish.

I have faith in you!

Now, take your hands and clap them together behind your back. Put the book down and do it for three seconds. You should be able to clap approximately five to ten times in three seconds.

Do this now!

GOOD JOB.

That represents the people who are clapping for you, because you did it. You made the dream come true!

Didn't you hear the clap behind you?

That clap represents all the people who see how much you are growing right now!

The clap represents everyone who is behind your back and are supporting you, showing you their support by clapping for you!

YOU'RE UNSTOPPABLE. YOU ARE FREAKING AWESOME!

Now, continue to energize yourself by taking deep breaths all the way down into your diaphragm and feel how the oxygen kickstarts your creative force within and how it grows with each breath you take. Feel with each breath how your confidence grows, and how you become more and more confident in manifesting this little dream of yours, right here and right now.

11

LOBSTER

> *You are at it again! Yes, of course you are. You do not give up. You are resilient. You are powerful, and you are proving it by taking action again and again.*

Now, let me ask you this question: is love important?

Yes, you are right, of course love is important. You deserve to love and to be loved. But, how important is love to give, show, and receive?

There is one study I want to tell you about, because it is relevant in this chapter. This study was performed in the 1940s. It was conducted because it was baffling how many small babies were dying in orphanages at the time. The theory was that these babies were dying because the environment was not sterile enough. It was believed that they were infecting each other and getting sick and dying. Because this was just speculation, Australian Rene Spitz decided to study it further. She started to monitor and observe babies in several orphanages, and to prove that this might be caused by un-cleanliness, she also monitored babies in several prisons, where the mothers went into the prisons pregnant and had their babies in prison and raised their babies there.

Thirty-seven percent of the children who were monitored in the orphanages died, but not one death was recorded in the filthy prisons. When she started to draw her conclusions from the study, she saw that the babies in orphanages were left lying alone in bed with little to no human contact during their stay. The environment was clean enough, but they received no love. Consequently, thirty-seven percent of them died, and that's near half of them. Thirty-seven percent of the babies died because they did not receive enough love.

> *You know how important love is in your life and how important it is to show love.*

I am using this study as reference for the left-brainers out there reading this book, who need to know the statistics behind the fact that we all need to be loved.

WE ALL KNOW THAT LOVE IS VERY IMPORTANT.

We all want to be loved, and we all want to love.

Of course, there are people out there who have been kept away from love or who have tried to convince themselves they do not need love and have actively been creating their reality based on their limited believe that they do not need to love or be loved.

Love is the fourth highest energy vibration level that we humans can reach, as far as we know. When you're at the energy vibration level of love, you can affect up to 750,000 people in a positive way, simply with the energy you send out to the universe with your vibration.

But what if you become desperate?

What if you start to give love because you desperately need love?

How does the vortex of love work?

The vortex works like this, the more you give love, the less you need love from others, and as a result of not needing it, you receive more love.

Once again, you see that there are many things in life that work in reverse. The vicious cycle of love is such that the more you love, the more you are loved.

But if you are desperate for love, how can you do this now?

You really need it, and you start to give and give with that mindset, and in return, you get almost no love back.

Why does it work like that?

This is pretty easy to explain: when you put your attention on the lack of or wanting something, when you are giving love with a mentality of the lack of love, that is exactly what you get back, more lack of love. You start to give with the mindset of wanting love, and the universe says:

> *I understand you, you want love, that's the feeling you are sending out. Let me help you out, I'll send you greater lack of love immediately.*
>
> *You're welcome!*
>
> *Here you go, your wish is your command.*
>
> *Your feelings of lack are your command, I will increase it for you.*
>
> *I will give you more of it.*

How do you show your love and how do you want to experience love?

This is a question you may ask yourself often. Suppose you currently have thousands of followers, and you are speaking on stages around the world. You love your followers, and you love the fact that your lectures inspire and educate people, by giving them tools and techniques to become the best version of themselves. You are changing lives.

You stand behind the stage ready to go and talk to 2,000 people who are waiting, excited to see you. You are their role model in life. You become nervous about your presentation. You are worried that you will not look good enough on stage. Worried about the fact that something might go terribly wrong. You might stutter on the stage, or you might even forget what to say. The technology might malfunction, and you might look bad on stage. You are building up resistance and mental blocks inside of yourself.

Now comes the question, who is the love intended for with this attitude?

Is it true love you have for you followers, or is it all one big self-deception, a delusion?

Is the lecture intended for them or for you?

If they receive the message, does it matter what you look like on stage?

Exactly, you are right; it's all about helping them. This is not about you, but about how you can get the message to them. It's all about how much influence you can have on your audience. Let's put this in perspective. Imagine you witness a car rolling over into a ditch on your way to the lecture, and while you are trying to help the family escape from their vehicle, a car pulls up to the crash site. It's the news van. The reporters start to film as you are trying your best to save this family. Should you fix your hair, or clean the dirt off your arm now, or maybe polish your shoes? Which is more important, to save the family or to look good on TV? When you help others, it's never about you. You show your love the best way possible by letting people feel that you genuinely do care about what happens to them and not so much about how you will look on stage.

Self-confidence is great. Combining both self-confidence and giving selflessly is a masterful combination.

People feel good to know that you love helping them so much that if they do not come to your events, you feel like you have failed them. You know you're the best coach in the world for them and that your contribution makes a huge difference in their journey. You are not full of yourself; you are just confident and know that you can help them. This is the attitude your clients want to experience when they seek your help.

Here is yet another example of how the world works in opposites. When you give your love unselfishly, with no expectations nor demands that they love you in return, that's when you get the most love back.

When your focus is on giving love, then, you will receive exactly that from the universe, a gift of love. You get the most out of your training when you do this right, give without expecting something in return, because you get so much more back.

Can we then assume you are doing this all for you, if you get the most back by doing it that way?

That's a really good question for you to think about. For whom are you doing all of this? Is this all because you really love yourself so much? Think about it: you are me, and we are all one; we are all connected. Is it being unselfish or is actually being selfish to give love without expecting anything in return, knowing you get the most back this way? This is a just a philosophical question for you to ponder.

This may come as a surprise, but you often need to make a plan when comes to delivering your love to people. You can have a general plan in your head, but sometimes, you need to sit down and write how you're going to do it. Make some sort of a love strategy. Yes, although we are talking about feelings like love, you must decide where, when, and how you are going to show them that you love them. Sit down and write it out, and decide to share your love.

Does that not sound practical or sexy to you?

Who cares?

Do you care?

No, you don't care; you would not have that mindset after everything you have been through. You understand that many things that you must do to make your life happier or to love more are often things that you might refer to as unpractical or unsexy. Writing down your plan, even when it comes to showing feelings, works incredibly well. The power of writing something into existence has been recognized for a very long time.

For example, let's say you're still in doubt that you can simply decide to become happier. Today, start writing down all the events in your life where you experienced happiness. I will continue with this example and make a list, as a guess, that might apply to you. Even though I take a few examples here, you should write down your own list of events when you were extremely happy.

I was happy on my birthday, at Christmas, when I went abroad last summer, and when I meet my friends from high school or from work — we always have so much fun when we meet, and I am really happy.

Let's take a moment and look at these events. For now, let's say that these are the events you will write down or that you just wrote down on your paper.

What do all these events have in common?

Most of them have been decided as happy moments before you experience them. None of these moments surprised you, nothing unexpected. You knew that you would be happy when the moment came. Do you get what I am saying here? Just like you know by now that you will feel great when you continue reading the next chapter in this book. The great feeling starts, even before you start reading. It starts as soon as you decide to pick up the book. Your brain says,

Oh yeah, we are about to get some constructive positive content and some praises. Let's get the party started!

Once you start to open the book without having read anything at that point, you are already starting to feel better and happier, because your brain is already pumping out endorphins throughout your body.

You've decided that you will feel great while reading the next chapter based on your previous present moments. You have already decided that you will be happy while reading and learning more.

The same thing applies to Christmas or meeting up with your friends: you start to feel better before the event starts. Acting on the things you know will bring you happiness is the one of the keys to well-being in your life.

You know you're happy right now.

You decided it.

Once you figure this out, understand it, and implement it as often as possible, there is no turning back: you will have more and more happiness and love in your life.

> ***Know beforehand that you will be happy, by deciding it before the event starts, and you will be happy.***

Hormones are what make you feel good — endorphins, dopamine, and serotonin. Your brain pumps these out into your body, and if you decide beforehand that you will feel great or be happy, it will have a great impact on your well-being and your happiness. Your brain will start to react before the event even starts.

Have you ever felt like the environment has too much control over you? Like society is prevent you from living a happy and fulfilled life?

Once upon a time, there was a young girl who said to her father that she was being controlled by her environment. She said that if she sees a problem and fixes it, she is simply creating another one. Therefore, she did not even see the point of trying. Her father, who was a chef, asked her to go with him into the kitchen, and he took out three pots. He then poured water into them and boiled the water in all three pots. He explained to her that we are all different. Some choose to let the environment shape us, while others don't. He then put eggs in one pot, potatoes in another, and coffee beans in the third one. After an hour in the boiling water, he turned off the heat and said, take a look! The potato was hard when it went into this environment, but became soft, the egg was soft when it went into the same environment, but became hard. Take a look at the coffee beans in the same environment; they changed the environment.

It does not matter what environment you are in now or have been in, what matters is how you experience it from the inside out. Do you react or respond? You either grow and flourish in your environment or shrink and slowly die. Today, there are people in the world who come from all kinds of environments and backgrounds, yet they succeed. We live in the era today when anyone can become successful. Think about that for a minute.

Your environment will ultimately affect you in some way in the long run. You can let the environment make you harder. You can let the environment turn you into a coward. You can change your environment. The fourth option is to leave your current environment that you're in and find an environment that supports your growth. The fourth option is often the best and easiest, especially when you feel you have outgrown the environment you live in.

> *Your environment is not just your location, but also the people you associate yourself with.*

For example, you don't need to move to another postal code to find a new environment; it can be done by associating yourself with a new crowd.

If you're anything like the lobster that has grown so much that it hurts to stay in the shell, which is now too small for you, you need to decide to squeeze yourself out of the small shell and hide behind a rock while you grow a new shell — a larger, better shell, a more beautiful shell, metaphorically speaking.

Have you already outgrown your current environment?

It is natural for the lobster to leave the shell when he has outgrown it, but for us humans, it is not so natural. You probably see people around you who have stopped growing because they are afraid to leave their small shell behind and become vulnerable while they grow a new, bigger shell, or, in other words, they are afraid to step outside their comfort zone. Those people stay in their small shell for the rest of their life, and therefore, they stop growing.

BUT NOT YOU!

You have come this far, and you are now in the position of having the knowledge and courage to grow for the rest of your life, as long as you want to.

When you start spending time with people who support your growth, it's the same as leaving your small shell behind. The same as moving into a new environment. This is not the literal meaning of moving house, although that's fine as well. It's about surrounding yourself with people whom you can learn from and you feel good around. People who influence you in a good way.

For example, choose to surround yourself with people who have a positive influence on you, who are positive on social media, and start hanging around other people at work who you did not think you were compatible with before. Now, you are interested in learning about the real estate investments that he or she has always been talking about, but you avoided in the past. Start spending time with your uncle. You know — the one who is the most successful in your family. Listen to him, show genuine interest in his ventures, learn as he speaks about them, and ask questions. Most people love to talk about their wins, what they are doing, and what they have done. When you start to ask questions with enthusiasm, he becomes more enthusiastic himself and starts to tell you about his wins, his traveling experiences, and his ventures, and you listen with great attention, because you know by now that you can create your own reality like you want to experience it.

You know you have no limits.

YOU KNOW YOU ARE FREAKING AMAZING.

I do want to emphasize that when you hear me saying that you are amazing and awesome, it's the truth! The truth is that we are all one, we are all connected, and if I'm amazing, you are, too. That's exactly why I can say without a doubt that you are amazing. That is why I can say that you are great and that you can do anything you want to achieve.

Stay focused on the big things in your life, the things that matter most to you. Don't get caught up focusing too much on all the small details all the time. Don't not let life pass you by when you have your attention on the small things all the time. Think about the big picture and the big important things in your life first, and then, the small details. Set your priorities right, and love as much as you want and can.

Just be you, the awesome human that you are, and keep making this world a better place with your smile.

Go ahead and smile!

GO AHEAD, SMILE :)

You know it feels great and rewarding to smile, even with no particular reason to smile. You do not need a reason!

Just send a big smile out to the universe!

Smile and enjoy experiencing yourself.

Enjoy and use a few seconds to experience how wonderful it feels to smile without a reason and grow in this moment by being you, right here and right now.

12

OBSESSED

> *Awesome, you are back at it again. It's great to know that you have enough energy today to pick up where you left off and keep feeding your brain. Yes, feeding your brain! It's when you strain the brain or learn something new to become a better version of yourself.*

What happens when you tell yourself a lie often enough?

How many times do you have to lie to yourself before it becomes your truth?

When does something go from being a lie to being your new true reality?

This can both be a bad thing and good thing, depending on how you use it. If there is no positive truth to what you are lying to yourself about, this is bad, because it won't be long until you start to believe this new truth, usually sooner that you think.

This can be great if, for example, you do not believe you are truly this freaking amazing being that I know you are. Then, you can use the method of repeating that to yourself daily, which you might consider a lie today, and turn it into your new reality, your new truth. Repeat it as often as possible, the affirmation of what you want your reality to be.

Your mind is amazing, and so are you. You are perfect. Never forget that you are the most perfect creation on earth. You were born to create.

It's amazing how this vehicle of yours works, your mind, body, and soul. It's incredible when we allow ourselves to wonder about the human vehicle and how it works! We are perfect; you are perfect.

It is unbelievable that we are such perfect beings, that you are such a perfect being and, yet, we tend to focus on our flaws.

YOUR BODY IS A WORK OF ART.

Do you appreciate and treat your body with the respect?

It is not enough to know what you should be doing. Are you doing it?

Are you treating your body with respect and love?

As perfect as your vehicle is, you are fundamentally flawed as well. **You are an addict!** Whether you are an active addict or believe yourself to be inactive, there is something that has too much control of your life right now, and you know it! Sometimes, you create problems on purpose, difficulties, arguments, or conflicts to be able to say to yourself, *Wow, now I deserve or need this thing!*

What is that thing that has too much control over you?

What is this thing that controls your life too much, to a certain extend? Is it food, sweets, attention, social media, nicotine, TV, alcohol, or drugs maybe? What's controlling your behavior so much right now that if you would take back the control right now, people would see a change in your behavior, and some people close to you would even notice a change in your personality? What is the addiction that popped into your mind just then, the addiction that not only affects your behavior, but your personality, as well?

Have you sold yourself the idea that everything is fine, that there is someone worse than you? What arguments do you use to justify this addiction just before you let your addiction take control, once again?

Do you allow yourself to think you have everything under control and that this is just something that you want to be doing, or do you not know why this thing has this much control over your reality? Do you know that all addiction can be traced back to the fact that you just want to be happy, that you want to be loved and treated well?

It's not really that complicated, but you have managed to complicate this throughout your life, over and over again. Most of us have.

Well done! I don't say that to offend you, we all need to wake up, look inward at our higher self, and let go of our ego to realize that we no longer control some aspect of our lives and that we are not creating the reality we want while we are still under the control of whatever it is that has a grip on our reality and we do not want to let go of it. Yes, that's right, you do not want to let go; it's much easier to cruise through life and let your addiction control you, rather than taking back the control and managing your desires without addiction. You might feel a bit lost when you finally decide to take back control and regain all your creative power.

It's pretty difficult to read and to think about this subject. It can be incredibly difficult to realize what it is that has too much control over your life and, yes, it does not matter what it is that you have been using as a crutch in life. Something that has too much power over your reality than it needs to have. It could be something seemingly innocent, like watching a lot of TV, which has a grasp on your reality. Perhaps, you are addicted to get as far away from your own reality as often as you can and experience the absence of your own reality through films and TV shows, zoned out with your brain in alpha mode. This addiction is something that impacts your life: you are slowly but surely wasting your life on this addiction. Alcohol, drugs, tobacco, or sugar, it does not matter what you're addicted to, you're slowly wasting your time and not growing while you lean against your addiction, and you're taking away your free will by letting your addiction control you, however small or big it is.

Do you want to stop? Do you want to overcome your habit or addiction, or have you not done enough damage yet?

Have you not slowed your growth long enough?

Have you not become ill from whatever your addiction is?

Are you waiting to reach the bottom, waiting for a note from the doctor that states you have only so long to live?

How far do you need to go with your thing, before you feel the need to change it, before you are ready to change your reality and take back control? Those who are addicted to drugs sell themselves the idea, *At least I'm not snorting drugs*, or, at the least, *I am not shooting myself up*. The alcoholic has 1,000 excuses.

I never drink on weekdays.

I never get hungover.

I only drink when I want to.

If drinking is so bad as some people are saying, why is it not illegal, like drugs?

I can handle my drinking.

The first step is to identify if you have something in your life that controls your reality or not.

The next step is to realize what that is and how it affects your actions, how this addiction controls everything or parts of your life, directly or indirectly.

When you have identified what it is and how it's affecting your reality, the next step is to seek help.

If you think you do not need any help, ask yourself this question: if you know it's not good for you and that it is limiting your growth, why are you still doing it? If you do not need help, why have you not stopped doing it already?

If you are going to stop doing that thing, right now, today, the worst thing you can do is to stop that thing and hold your breath while you wait for the craving to fade from your reality. The best thing you could do is to replace your addiction with a healthy addiction or obsession. Something you can be obsessed about that supports your growth.

What is a healthy obsession anyway?

- It could an obsession with success!
- To be obsessed and addicted to the hormones that are released from the brain when you help people.

- Being obsessed with receiving compliments and, therefore, you put all your effort and obsession into creating products or services that helps people grow and flourish, creating a situation where people are constantly complimenting you.

- Addiction to become better.

- Addiction to experience more.

- The obsession to find and become one with the light inside of you and to use this creative power within you to get closer to the light and create opportunities to experience whatever supports your growth on your journey.

- Addiction to experiencing the energy of nature and the energy within you. The desire to experience as much as you possibly can in this life.

- Even addiction to adrenaline can be positive, although that kind of addiction could lead you to dangerous situations in your life, lol.

Have you sought help?

Have you admitted to yourself that you have an addiction of any kind, or are you still convincing yourself how much you deserve whatever you have been leaning up against and using as a crutch?

I deserve to treat myself now, because I did great here or there, or maybe, *I am such a victim I need this or that now.*

Did you know that one of the biggest reasons for addiction can be traced directly to social isolation? When case studies on sugar and heroin addiction have been done on rats, this becomes clearly evident. When rats are social, when you place a rat with many others rats and let them play together and associate with other rats, the rat never becomes an addict. When they are alone and isolated from other rats, this is almost always the opposite. The rat becomes an addict, and she will start using heroin until she eventually kills herself from the addiction.

Now, take a moment to think about what a huge difference this is. In both cases, the rats have unlimited access to heroin around the clock, but, when they are in a social setting, they leave the heroin alone, and when isolated, they becomes addicts and take their new job, as addicts, so seriously that they kill themselves from the use of heroin. Sugar addiction is also connected to social isolation.

Associate yourself around people who help you grow. Don't isolate yourself. It's very hard to control your bad habits in isolation.

When humans use drugs, we are seeking happiness, and when we use, we start drawing happiness from our happy account at the happy bank without ever making a deposit. We sneak inside the backdoor, so to speak, with severe consequences.

When you pass an ATM today, why don't you stop by to withdraw some money? Not from your current account, but from a new account. But, wait, you might be thinking right now, new accounts are empty, right? There have not been any deposits made, how can I withdraw from the new account with no balance? You are absolutely right, yet, when we are communicating with other human beings, we are quite willing to make a withdrawal without ever making a deposit.

We jump on the opportunity to ask for a favor without having brought anything of value into their lives.

The same could be said when we are trying to build new business relationships.

DON'T TRY TO MAKE A WITHDRAWAL BEFORE YOU MAKE A DEPOSIT.

Where else do we make withdrawals with no balance?

Maybe the best example of that is when we use mind-altering drugs that change our perception. Then, we are withdrawing happiness. Or even with certain substances, we can get to experience a closer relationship with the light within, without having worked for it, without making a deposit. What happens when we make a withdrawal from the bank on an empty account?

Overdraft, interest rates, fees, fines, transaction fees, and even terminated accounts in some cases. You understand all of this very well when it comes the bank, but are you still trying to make withdrawals without making a deposit first, when it comes to your happiness?

Do you have any checks in the bank of happiness that have bounced, and the bank is still waiting on your deposits to settle your accounts?

This chapter is not about taking anything from you in one way or another. This is about you deciding when you are going to start to fulfill your purpose, the purpose you choose yourself, the day you arrived in this world, or maybe even sooner.

When are you going stop making deposit-free withdrawals from your happiness accounts?

When will you stop making withdrawals from your account in the bank of time without a deposit?

When are you going to pull yourself together and start realizing that you deserve to experience life in ecstasy you create for yourself, not with sugar, alcohol, drugs, tobacco, or any other addictions that control your actions and fate?

You have experienced enough to stop believing in a magic pill that will give you the experience you desire every day.

When will be the right time for you to stand up and say:

This is enough. Now, I'm going to take back control of my life and start experiencing what I choose. I am going to be happy! I am going to love. I'm going to create my reality, so that can live each day experiencing as much as possible, and so that I can live my life in a state of love, a state of euphoria. I'm happy. I am love. I love myself. I love my body, and I make good decisions that benefit my whole vehicle. I create my own life. I create my own reality. I have had enough of living my live for others, living for my addiction, and now my time has come. I am ready. Bring it on, mister universe, bring on all those things I might have interpreted as difficulties yesterday and used to excuse my addiction. Bring it, I am ready. I am ready to experience and start influencing others by leading by example. I'm so ready to become the person I choose to be when I decided to be born here. I am a creator, and I have finally realized that I am ready! I am love!

Now, take some time by yourself and take in what you have just read. Maybe you have already taken back all the control by now. If you have, I would like to applaud you.

YOU ARE SUPER-FREAKING AMAZING.

Your task of the day, is to call or contact one person who you have neglected or who you have been wanting to say you are sorry to. Remember that no matter how much or how little you put into your forgiveness, there is someone who needs to hear it. If that person tries to make your apology seem like a small thing or tries to convince you that it's not necessary, remember, it's a big step for you.

When you are done, you should also contact one person you need to thank for something. The same applies to this person; it does not matter the size of the matter you are thanking him or her for. Regardless whether you are thanking them for saving your life or helping you move house ten years ago, or even for a birthday gift. Thank that person for something that you remember you have not done yet.

You are the one who will get the most out of these conversations. This is for you, you must do this, you made a commitment to yourself when you picked up this book, and you will never forget the time you spend on these tasks that gave you the ability to continue to grow and start taking full responsibility of your life. If this is your second time reading this book, then you need to find another person to thank and to say sorry to. That's how you keep growing. Learn, take action, grow, repeat and grow some more.

YOU ARE GREAT, AND YOU ARE FREAKING AMAZING.

You might not have anything in your life you need to stop doing right now, and if so, you are doing an amazing job with your life right now and deserve a big compliment on your achievement. Nothing in this chapter was an attack on you in any way, most of us have something that we need to identify and change, to take a gigantic leap forward in our growth. If you have identified anything in your life that you realize has too much control and are ready to change it, then great job. You are amazing!

Now, take a few deep breaths in, all the way into your diaphragm, and when you let each breath go, think about releasing what has been holding you back. Each out breath symbolizes letting something go that has too much control over your reality, and now, you are changing it. Do this now, and feel how much control you are taking back in your life, right here and right now.

13

WE ARE ONE

> *Great job! Exceptionally nice work from you so far!*

Go ahead and pat yourself on the shoulder, because you have earned it. You have decided to seize the day. Yes, it's you who is deciding it and doing it. It is you who is making this possible! You are taking action, you are growing and seeing more and more success in the things you act on in your reality.

Congratulations on being the freaking amazing person you are!

You are unique, and your contribution to this day is unique.

There is no one who can be better at being you than you.

Remember that your contribution to this world matters!

You are the only person with exactly your experience and qualities, and the world needs you.

Now, take a couple of deep breaths, and breathe in this beautiful day. The beauty is undeniable if you just look.

Do this now!

Decide now that you are going to see all the beauty this day has to offer. It will give you plenty to smile about.

Pay close attention to all the people who cross your path today. Send them a smile. Show them that you are alive. Allow yourself to give something of yourself. Be the best you and enjoy giving of yourself, by allowing people to feel you. We are all connected, and when you feel it and experience it, it gives you pleasure. Sensing and experiencing that your contribution to this world matters.

When you see the next person who crosses your path today, pay close attention, because that person is you. You can actually only see yourself reflected in others. When you admire a person, you are really admiring yourself. Which is, perhaps, no wonder, because you are so freaking awesome! Smile! Yes, you are freaking awesome!

You may possibly not have adapted these qualities yet within you, but you will. When you judge something in others, you are judging something you identify in yourself in that person. Perhaps a dark side of you or a part of you that you do not want recognize. The more you agree with your ego, your lower self, the more you will judge both yourself and others. Today, you can embrace the fact that you can take full responsibility for your life and experience greater awareness and awakening in your reality and start embracing the truth that we are all one.

Now, shift your attention to your legs! How are they touching the ground or the inside of your shoes? Take a few seconds and just experience it now!

How are you breathing right now?

Now, you are going to take a full, conscious breath, all the way down into your diaphragm and fill up your chest. Imagine that you are pouring water in a bottle as you breathe. Begin to fill up the air at the bottom of your stomach, and then, work your way up to your chest. When you blow the oxygen back out, start by emptying your breast first, and then, finally, push out all the air from your stomach. Now, we are going to do this together, and when we do this, visualize that you are breathing in pure, white healing light. Feel with each breath how your body gets lighter and you start to feel better. Once you have fully inhaled, visualize how your entire body is filled with pure white light. We are going to release as much of your stress and anxiety out of your body as you allow yourself to release with your out breath.

Now, put your attention and intention on your breathing as we start to breath consciously together three times now.

Take a full breath in, stomach first, good, and then, fill up the chest, and visualize the pure white light spreading all over the body as you hold your breath.

Wait three seconds.

Now release it! Great job!

Do it again now! In at the bottom first and, then, the chest. Visualize and hold it.

Wait three seconds.

Now, let it go! Yes, great job!

And once more, draw a deep breath from the bottom and up, visualize and hold it.

Wait three seconds.

Now, let go again on top first and, finally, empty your stomach!

Great job! Good breath work and visualization!

Now, I'm going to ask you to read these ten affirmations out loud. If you can't do it out loud, move to somewhere you can.

1. Happiness is my birthright.
2. I feel joy and pleasure in this moment right now.
3. I love life, and I wake up interested in life.
4. I can look within, into my fountain of inner happiness, whenever I wish.
5. By allowing myself to be happy, I lead by example for others to follow.
6. I look at the world and can't help but feel joy and smile.
7. I feel joy and pleasure in the simple tasks of life.
8. I have a sense of humor and love to share laughter with the world.
9. My heart flows with joy.
10. When I go to bed, I can rest happy, knowing that all is well in my reality.

Good job, saying it out loud has massive effects on your life, and, of course, you know that by now. Now, give yourself ten seconds to think about something that pleases you.

Do that now!

WHAT MAKES YOU SMILE?

Start doing more of what pleases you! Doing more of what makes you happy! You are so incredibly super-amazing when you are happy!

You are dependent upon your thoughts.

You have countless thoughts a day. Many of those thoughts do not serve you. Thoughts that do not support you in being the person you want to be.

If you could create a new you from scratch, how would this new you be?

Have you put any thought to that?

Some thoughts have often come to you, and you have given them your attention, and that's why they have become a part of your reality. Many thoughts that you have given you attention to, that you think about again and again, those thoughts have been keeping you from the growth that you have been working towards. Reliving a memory, especially bad ones, trigger the same gene expression as the actual incident did. Thinking and visualizing bad scenarios can trigger the same effect. The brain does not know the difference between a thought and the actual event, if you experience the emotions associated with that action or event.

Think about what you will accomplish when you adapt new thoughts, better thoughts, that serve you in creating the reality you truly want.

When the old thoughts that do not serve you appear, let them pass through. Remember that they are not yours unless you give them your attention.

> ***Unwanted manifestation happens when you give unwanted thoughts your attention. Let them pass through!***

Practice makes perfect! You can take control and be your own creator. Create your reality, your life, just like you want it to be, simply by changing the way you think. Changing which thoughts you give your attention.

> ***Did you know that you can control and choose the thoughts that you want to think?***

Lets put it to the test, think about the word dolphin.

Say the word dolphin with your inner voice, now!

Say the word dolphin, in your head very loud! Scream the word in your head, as though you were trying to yell at someone far away.

Dolphin, hey dolphin!

Do it right now!

Now, say your favorite color in your head, very loud as well. Scream it in your head.

Now, say your favorite color ten times, as fast as you can, in your head.

Please pay attention to the difference when you choose your thoughts just like you did just now and when you give unwanted thoughts your attention. When you choose which thoughts to think and which thoughts you give your attention to, you are consciously manifesting the reality you want.

Do you see the difference?

Do you feel the difference?

You may stub your toe or spill a glass of milk, and you might choose to think something along these lines:

Great! Now look what you did, what else could go wrong today, why does this always happen to me?

Did you choose those thoughts, or did they simply appear?

Is there a difference when you choose to think something and when you do not?

Yes, there is a distinct difference, and you feel it.

With tens of thousands of thoughts you get each day, which of them did you really choose? How many did you choose, like when you just chose to think about your favorite color?

How many of these involuntary thoughts are thought patterns or old, subconscious habits?

How many of those thoughts are old programs that still live in your reality?

Today, practice classifying which thoughts serve you and which don't. Ask yourself how you feel with this thought, about this thought. How does this particular thought that has come to you make you feel?

Does it make you feel good, or does it paralyze you?

If it does not serve your growth, let it pass through and, instead, linger on the thoughts that please you and serve your growth. Give them all your attention.

When you train your thought flow and start taking control of your thought patterns, it is very important to choose the thoughts that please you and support your growth. By doing that, you start to own your thoughts, and not the other way around.

YOU ARE FREAKING AMAZING!

It is important to get as much control as possible over your thought patterns and learn how you can trigger happy thoughts whenever you need it or want to change your mood. You have full control over your life, over your reality, and full control of how you feel and want to feel.

YOU ARE THE CREATOR OF YOUR OWN REALITY!

Happiness is a choice! It's a state of mind! It's your mindset. It's hormones that are released throughout your body. You have the control, if you practice it and master it. It's a choice!

Decide to be happy right now, if you haven't already! Make the decision to do everything in your power to be happy. As soon as you decide to be happy, the universe will start to cooperate with you. The universe will start to present events, people, and situations that support your decision. You have a light inside of you, and this light awaits your decision to be able to start shining brightly. It's time to start letting your light shine. Enlightenment is the process of finding that light within and starting to know what you are and what you are not. Just be you, and nothing else, and live in the state of emotional certainty.

Now, your role is to realize that you are more. You are much more than this body of yours.

You are amazing!

You are a creator.

You can do anything you want to do.

You can change your reality into whatever you like.

You can decide to look at everything you have already manifested into your life and say, "Yes, I did this," no matter what it is. Nothing you do or think is right nor wrong.

The question is, what do you want to create in your reality?

What do you want to manifest from this day forward?

You create your own luck, you were born to create!

YOU ARE A FREAKING AMAZING CREATOR.

You have your inner voice that is constantly talking to you. What is this voice saying?

Have you been listening to this inner voice?

This is your inner navigator. This voice will bring you to where you want to go. This is your soul calling you. We were put on this earth to find ourselves again. To remember who we are. But when we became adults, we allowed our inner child to die inside of us. We were raised to listen to old ideas, what society wants from us, what society wants you to be and does not want you to be. Now, it is time to reclaim your inner child and comfort it back to life and allow it to flourish. Let the inner child come out and play. Allow yourself to be exactly as you want to be. Throw questions out there, and allow your soul to answer. Allow your instincts to lead you forward.

NOTHING IS ACCIDENTAL.

There is message for you everywhere, if you just stay focused and pay attention. Then, you will see them. The universe is constantly guiding you in one way or another. It is up to you to decide to listen and see.

WE ARE ALL CONNECTED, WE ARE ALL ONE.

Now try standing up, and walk backwards a few steps. Do something you're not used to doing. Reset yourself. Do it to snap yourself out of the old programming and into the awareness that there is more, not just the same thing over and over again. When you walk backwards, do it slowly, with full awareness — make sure you do it as safely as possible. Keep walking backwards for a few steps, and do not let your mind tell you that you cannot, because you can. Decide to do it anyway; go backwards. Who cares if someone sees you? Think of yourself and no one else right now. This is for you, just like the reality you are constantly creating — it's just for you.

Put the book down, and do this now!

Did you enjoy that? Did you think it was difficult? If so, was it difficult for you physically, or difficult to step outside your comfort zone?

It is quite normal either way, especially if this is something you have not done for a long time, maybe not since you were a child. You did do it, right? All these simple exercises are what make this book come alive, and they all play a role in your shift, in your transformation. There is not one exercise in this book that does not serve a purpose!

Adulthood often means that people stop playing. Forget about that now; it is time to start playing again. Let your inner child shine.

Now, pick something up around you: a stone, a pen, a crystal, or any object that is close by you right now.

Examine it.

How does it feel when you touch it?

Is it cold or warm?

What shape is it: circular, square, or something else?

Is it broken or whole?

Enjoy being there in the now with all your attention on this object.

Then, take in your surrounding environment for a minute and find a new home for this object. Close your eyes and ask where its new home is, and put it down where your instincts tell you it should be. Go with you first impression.

Be completely in the moment, and enjoy this game! This is a very simple and fun game to practice listening to your intuition.

Do this now!

You have done extremely well today.

Now, take in what you just read in this chapter and what you experienced doing the exercises.

> *Enjoy being you, because you are freaking awesome, right here and right now.*

14

ENERGY

> *Are you fired up today?*
> *Are you proud of yourself?*

You must be, and you should be. I certainly am! I am so proud of you, because you have been absolutely fantastic so far. You have managed to surprise yourself with your dedication and willpower. You have proven that you are energetic, positive, and open to new ideas. You are willing to follow instructions and implement what you have been learning, stepping outside your comfort zone, and slowly, but surely, becoming a better you each day.

By following and implementing what you have been reading, you are part of the top two percent of people in the world. Did you know that? It's easier than you think to be in the top two in the world. Putting this in perspective, according to figures from Tony Robbins in 2017, 66 percent of the world population had to survive on less than $2.50 a day. That's less than $80 each month.

If you have more than $80 each month to survive on, you are already in the top 30 percent. You have it pretty good when you put it perspective to the whole world. You are most likely in the top two percent or at least very close to it. Therefore, it is often difficult for you to understand the problems others are facing in the world. Your life is really good. Yes, no matter what salary you have right now, you are very likely to be somewhere close to the top one or two percent in the world. You are in the top one percent of the people who are ready to take in new ideas and implement them to shift your reality. Your growth in your personal development journey is in the top one percent. You are a top-one-percent personality.

Do you have any negative energy or feelings you want to get rid of today?

Do you want to release them right now?

Let's do that now, before we start talking about energy and how your energy can influence others and even how you can affect your food with your energy vibration. Now, we are going to release any bad energy from you that you want to rid yourself of: frustration, worry, anger, sadness, or even disbelief. Go ahead and select the feeling you want to get rid of right now.

Think about what has been bothering you these past few days — or even longer, for that matter — whatever it is that does not make you feel good.

Do you have it in your mind now what it is that you want to get rid of?

Good, now take your hands and put them together, as if you were holding a young chick in your hands. Put them together, and hold the imaginary chick in your hands carefully, so the chick does not fall out of your palms. Hold the chick with your palms up in the air and between your thumbs, place you mouth over the hole and whisper the opposite of what you don't want to feel into your palms right now.

You may feel you haven't been looking your best, you might feel you are not fresh, or you might have been experiencing some inferiority complexes. Now, whisper into your palms exactly the opposite. Let's use the example that you don't feel like you are looking your best today. Whisper it into my palms:

I feel fantastic about my appearance today.

Say whatever is opposite of the feeling you want to change into a positive. When you are done whispering the opposite of what you want to get rid of, close your palms completely, and hold it in your closed palms for a few seconds. If you have not been feeling so energetic lately, whisper:

I am unusually energetic today.

Then, close your palms and keep it in there for a few seconds. Now, put the book down, and take 20 seconds to whisper as many opposites as you want in the palms of your hands. The opposite of what you want to get rid of.

Do this now!

Now, you should have all your positive changes in your closed palms in front of you, and all you want is in your hands now. Now, take your hands and toss it all up into the universe. As you toss it out into the universe, say this out loud:

Take this gift. This is my gift to the universe. Take my feelings I have placed in my palms and multiply it, thank you!

Do this now!

Now, repeat these four short sentences out loud:
> Forgive me!
> I'm sorry!
> I love you!
> Thank you!

This is a simple exercise that allows you to take full responsibility of your life and even others. While you say these sentences out loud, think about what you want to take full control over in your reality.

Repeat these sentences three times, now!

This exercise allows you to take full responsibility when you are angry at someone or want to take responsibility for someone you care about. You can also use it when you feel you have no control over your environment or the events unfolding in your reality. This exercise can be used on anything you want to take responsibility for. I recommend you try it and find out how it works for yourself. The next time you do not feel good about something in your reality, repeat these four sentences while thinking about that topic, and repeat them until you feel you can take full responsibility for those events or person. Try it, and see what happens. Just keep repeating those four short sentences. The order of the sentences does not matter at all. Just keep repeating them, until you feel the change, until you feel the shift. You will know when it happens. Listen to your body, and feel when the shift happens. This is like anything else: you need to use it on a regular basis to see the effect it will have on your life. This is a well-known exercise called Ho'oponopono.

It's amazing how you raised your energy vibration with this simple exercise. It is amazing how simple words can make you feel more energetic than you did before.

Have you ever ordered food in a restaurant that was exactly the same as you have tried to make yourself, but the food tasted twice as good, or vice versa? Have you cooked something yourself that you have been served at a restaurant before, but your food tasted so much better? How is it possible that food can taste better when one person makes it than when another person prepares the same food with the same ingredients and the same recipe?

Do you know the reason?

It is because you put your energy into the food with each ingredient you handle. If you have negative energy that day, the food will not taste as good, and it will not be as healthy. If you have positive energy, you will feel the difference, and everyone who gets to enjoy your meal benefits from your positive energy vibration.

Have you seen the movie called Like Water for Chocolate — or maybe you know it as its original name, Como Agua para Chocolate? In the movie, the main character bakes a wedding cake with a broken heart, and by accident, one of her tears fell into the mix. When the wedding guests ate the cake, they all ended up crying, because that is what she put into the cake. The tear is symbolic for the feelings that she was feeling. The energy she was vibrating from when she was baking the cake. Although this movie is fiction, there is a lot of truth behind this idea.

You have much greater impact on your food than you might have realized with the energy vibration you are sending out as you prepare the food and handle all the ingredients. This may sound unbelievable, and it is no coincidence I waited until this chapter to talk about this. This might have been hard to believe in the beginning, but, now, you have reached a place where, if you hear something that sounds unbelievable, you simply try it out, and find out for yourself how it works and if it works. You do not have to take anything as the absolute truth when you hear it for the first time, but, now, you have the knowledge and experience to not dismiss anything, either. Some things you know are true, even when you hear it for the first time — you can feel it in your DNA, in your gut — and other things you simply must find out if they work or not.

Around the year 1994, a man by the name of Masaru Emoto became obsessed with the idea that we do manipulate our food with our energy and influence everything in our environment. He began experimenting to find out whether they could possibly prove that our energy has this much effect on everything. They managed to prove the effect we have with our energy on water. They would freeze the water and, then, cut the ice into very thin slices and place them under a microscope to capture images of the frozen water crystals. I suggest you do a search online on the water crystal experiments and take a look at the beautiful images of these water crystals. The results from his studies are amazing. When a person said something beautiful to the water, such as I love you, the water crystals became extremely beautiful, but when they used hatred or such phrases as I will kill you, the crystals became terribly ugly and messy. Masaru Emoto did all kinds of experiments with the water. He had the water blessed, and they tried playing different kinds of music before freezing water, and the results directly reflected the music in the water crystals. Make sure you go and check the photos online and see the results for yourself.

Another man, Professor Dr. Brend Helmut Kröplin did similar studies on water. He wanted to see how the human consciousness and thoughts affect water, also known as water memory. They would dry the water drops after thinking different thoughts around the water, and the results are amazing. It has been scientifically proven that we have massive impact on the structure of water. What these studies demonstrate is that the human energy vibration has a direct influence on the structure of water, and we can see it directly in the water crystals and in the dried-out drops. We see what we put in there, and how we program the water with — words, music, actions, or thoughts.

Two other very similar experiments have been done in a double-blind study, both with blessed chocolate and blessed water. For the chocolate, they put the intention that the person who would eat it would feel extremely happy. Then, half of the participants got blessed chocolate and half regular, same brand, same source, without blessing. The results were as you might expect: more happiness eating the blessed chocolate. In the water experiment, they blessed half the water bottles, and then, they grew seeds from that water and measured the nutrition value and growth of the seeds. Once again, the proof was astounding. The seeds that got the blessed water — with the intention of better growth and more nutrition — saw better growth and more nutritional value.

A human being is about 60 percent water, and if you think you have not been affecting and shaping the people in your reality, you are mistaken. You certainly do. You change the structure of water every time you say something, do something, or think something.

YOU ARE INCREDIBLY POWERFUL.

You are constantly shaping this world.

> *Have you been carefully selecting your words, thoughts, and actions with the intention of creating a better, more beautiful world?*

Remember to think beautiful thoughts towards the food you cook and eat in your future, whether you believe this or not. Don't take any chances; what if this is actually true? No way, I don't think you would doubt this truth. Lol. You probably feel it in your gut already. What does your intuition tell you? Maybe you knew this all along? If you don't get a bad feeling in your gut, this is not something that comes as a surprise to you. You knew this already! However, you might not have heard it put into these words before, but, still, somehow, you already knew it.

YOU ARE AN INCREDIBLY AMAZING HUMAN BEING, AND YOU ALREADY KNOW THAT.

The next time you eat food, take a few seconds to say out loud or with your inner voice:

Who eats this food will benefit greatly and will feel an increase in their energy, health, wellness, and happiness.

You can browse the Internet for all kinds of research people have been doing at home, ordinary people speaking to a bowl of rice, for example. People who decided to try this out and not just blindly believe how our energy affects water and our food. If you look it up, you can see how when the food gets good energy, it lasts longer than food that gets bad energy. If, for any reason, you are skeptic at this point, you just have to try this out yourself. Sometimes, you just simply need to put your finger into the flame to feel the heat, despite the millions of people who have told you that fire will burn you. Some people just have to experience everything they are told. If that applies to you, do it tonight: experiment with food and your energy yourself. Do it with two identical jars. Put the same amount of water and rice in each jar, and close it. Each day, say something negative to one jar and something positive, like I love you, to the other jar, and see what happens. Of course, I have done this experiment, as well. It can be a lot of fun; if you have children, include them in the process.

Here, you can see the experiment I did with my daughter:

http://hunihunfjord.com/your-words-are-powerful/

One of the most remarkable men of all times was Nikola Tesla. He gave humanity many things that are still being used daily in the world today, like AC electricity, also called alternating currents, which is being used in most homes today. He invented radio receivers and broadcasters and the X-ray, to name a few.

But why mention him here? Because Tesla was obsessed with frequencies, like being able to send a certain frequency into the air and receive them somewhere else, like radio signals. Sending out a certain frequency and if the receiver is set to the same frequency, you can listen to the sound on the other side.

When you sit in your home later today, you should know that there is plenty of music in the room, and the reason why you don't hear it is because you not listening to the right frequency. Do you believe that or not? If you do not believe it, try it yourself. Pull out a radio if you have one, and start going through the frequencies, searching for radio stations that are broadcasting in your area. Start listening to how much music is already in your house. The radio did not pull the music into your house, it was already there. Your home contains a lot of music, but you didn't hear it until you started listening to the right frequency.

Tesla was obsessed with frequencies. All things and people have a specific frequency. If you are on the same frequency as another person, you are connected to that person; you can feel that person. This has been happening to you while reading this book, while gaining experience and doing the exercises in this book daily. You read and take in the information, learn, and take action. When you keep growing, you raise your energy vibration, your frequency, and then, you start to hear other people who you did not hear before.

Do you have anyone in your reality today who you are so connected to, that you feel if there is something wrong or if something is happening to the other person, bad or good? This connection is well-known with siblings, especially with twins, and it's also common for parents and their children to be connected on the same frequency. This type of connection between humans can be so strong that others have a hard time understanding it, unless they, themselves, have experienced such a connection.

You are always sending out energy, but the frequency changes according to the mood you are in, your state of mind, and what you are feeling. David Hawkins mapped the scale of consciousness. He mapped the level of our emotions, or, in other words, what energy level you are at when you feel a certain way. He basically mapped out how much influence you have on your environment at a specific emotional level. You are at your lowest frequency when you are in sorrow, feel shame, or feel guilt. Those feelings are all below 100 on the Hawkins scale. The scale starts at 20, at our lowest frequency level, to the highest known awareness level, which is at 1,000. You do not start to move any energy around you, until you reach about 150 on the scale, which is the state of anger. Love or being in love is at 500 on the scale, and in that state, you can affect up to 750,000 people in a positive way with your energy vibration. We have all experienced being in love or in the presence of someone in love. It is amazing to feel the energy and positive effects it has.

Here is something that might surprise you, though. On the scale of consciousness, when you let your inner child come out to play, when you are messing around, playing and having fun, you are vibrating at a higher energy frequency than love. When you let your inner child come out and play, you are at 540 on the scale.

So, the easiest way for you to have an enormous impact on the environment and the whole world is to allow your inner child to come out as often as possible, throw a snowball, swing, fart in the movie theater, make funny faces, ride a snowmobile, go horseback riding, go bowling, play with a child, finger paint, play with building blocks, or anything that makes you giggle and enjoy the moment. Have fun doing anything that makes your energy jump up to the point where you are in touch with your inner child.

The highest energy level you can reach is when you find the light within and become enlightened. It's when you connect and experience the source within. We all have a part of the source inside of us. You are part of everything. You are part of the creator, you are a creator. Enlightenment scores 700 to 1,000 on the scale of consciousness. Now, let's lighten up a bit. Let's not take life so seriously. The quickest way towards enlightenment is to lighten up.

ARE YOU SMILING? GO AHEAD, SMILE!

Now, take your index finger on one hand, and point it into the air. Anywhere you want to point it, just point it out there, and move it all over the place. Then, slowly start to let your index finger move like an airplane at an airshow. Let your finger move like an airplane all over the place.

Yes, just like that.

Now, just embrace your inner child for a minute, and let go.

Now, let the plane come towards your face and make a little airplane sound while you do it. Wuuumm.

Now, let the tip of your index finger touch your nose.

There it is, there's your nosy woozy, you found it, great job!

You are a fantastic energetic magical unicorn right now.

That was you, allowing yourself to let your inner child come out and play. This was you messing around. Well done, you either just raised your energy way up there, or you lowered it quite a bit, if you felt shame, embarrassment, or discomfort. If you allowed yourself to let go and step outside your comfort zone, letting your inner child come out to play and have a little bit of fun, you are now at 540 on a scale of consciousness. You are now at a higher energy vibrational level than when you are in the state of love.

> *You are amazing! Thank you for being so willing to learn! Thanks for daring to step outside your comfort zone, and thank you for making the world a better place.*

Now, take some time and just allow yourself to enjoy that feeling of allowing your inner child come out and play. Allow yourself to get childish thoughts and laugh out loud when you do something funny. Your laughter is contagious.

ARE YOU SMILING NOW?

Of course, you are. Of course, you are smiling, because you just found your nosy woozy, and you had been looking for you nosy woozy for a very long time, and there is was this whole time.

Feel how strong you are right now, being able to step outside the boundaries society has been trying limit you inside of all your life. You dared to let your inner child out, and for that, you are freaking amazing. Enjoy the feeling of being you, right here and right now.

15

YOUR GARDEN

YOU ARE FREAKING AWESOME!

You are absolutely awesome in everything you put your mind to. You are awesome, even when you fail. You are awesome, even when things don't go as planned! .

YOU ARE FANTASTIC, AND YOU KNOW THAT BY NOW!

You have taken the material that you have read here in this book and made it your own? Some of it, you have understood and, some, you have misunderstood, and that is all part of how awesome and interesting you really are. When you think about it, is it ever really possible to fail?

Do you know the answer?

The answer is, of course, no, you can't, because no matter what you experience, there is no right nor wrong, because you — and when I say you, I mean you, not you as you might think you are, but the true you — are here to experience yourself through what you think is you right now. Don't worry, I will explain what I mean later in the chapter.

How would it be possible to fail if your purpose is simply to experience and remember who you are? How can you fail, with free will?

Have you ever noticed anyone outside walking who is busy talking to themselves? You've probably seen this before and even caught yourself doing it. Not everyone goes so far as to speak out loud to themselves, but we are all having constant conversations in our minds. Isn't that true for yourself as well? Haven't you been having conversations in your mind? Contemplating something or just discussing what just happened? How you could have handled it better, and so on. Preparing yourself for the next meeting or conversation. Think about this for a second: if you can have a conversation in your mind, how many of you are in there?

How can you be talking to someone inside your mind?

PERHAPS, YOU ARE MORE THAN JUST YOUR MIND.

Where do your artistic talents come from?

They come from you — and I mean you, not from what you think is you. You might think that you are your mind, but it's just a device you use to experience yourself.

Do you understand what I mean?

Your mind is a tool that you use to experience your true self. You are your consciousness and you use the mind to experience yourself. The consciousness needs the mind to experience the past and the future, for example. Because there is no past or future, there is only the eternal present moment of now, right this instant is all you have. Yes, that is how it is: only the now.

> *The past is only a memory of the present moment and the future is only your imagination of what the present moment might look, be, and feel like.*

When the future present moment is here — tomorrow, for example — it will always come as the present moment. It is and always will be just the present moment, right now. Time is something your mind creates, so that you, the consciousness, can experience itself in the third dimension. Time is one of the things your consciousness needs in this world to experience itself. You sense time with your mind, with your rational thoughts. Your right brain processes the now, while your left brain processes memories, the past and projects a future, based on your knowledge and past present moments. This is why is so important to create your desired future by using you left brain to project a future. Then move it into the now, into the right brain and experience the future now, with all your senses and the right brain, therefore manifest it right now in the present moment as being already done.

Why do you think that scientists are often not artistic?

Why is it that scientists often have their biggest scientific breakthroughs during their breaks, away from the lab?

Why do they often get their epiphanies when they are not on the job?

I'll answer that for you. You might know the answer already. In fact, you *do* know the answer already — that is to say, you, the consciousness or higher self, knows the answer. Most people think they are their mind and/or thoughts.

Have you ever been able to be in the present moment without thinking, like, when you meditate?

Have you been able watch yourself without thought?

When you manage to clear out all your thoughts, you are you, the real you. The more you can turn off your thoughts, the more you get to experience happiness. The more you will experience the state of ecstasy, because without thought, you get closer to the light within you, and you get to experience the pure you in the present moment, in the now. In the state of no thought, your mind is not judging the future by the memories of your past present moments. In that moment, you are completely in the now, without a past or future, completely here in the now. You have no future or past, you just are.

The reason many scientists do not have artistic talent is that they can't consciously turn off their thoughts. Scientific discoveries often happen during breaks because the scientist accidentally turns off their thought for a split second, and that's when they get the answer they were seeking from the universal consciousness or from the field of all possibilities. From the field of higher intelligence or higher consciousness.

YOUR THINKING CLOUDS THE LIGHT INSIDE OF YOU, THE REAL YOU.

Your mind can be any way you choose it to be: you can be many, or just one. The question is whether you intend to let your mind who, by the way, thinks is you — stay in control, or if you want to allow yourself to remember and slowly, but surely, get closer to becoming one with the light. Enlightenment, as it is called, is really just you allowing yourself to experience you — the real you — more and more, by allowing yourself to experience what is there without any thought behind the thought. You have just forgotten who you are. But even when the sun is blocked by clouds, you still know it's there. It does not mean that the sun is no longer there, only that you cannot see it right now. Don't take life too seriously, though. Don't be afraid to let your inner child come out and play. In that state, is often where you are completely in the present moment, having fun.

> *The quickest way towards enlightenment is to lighten up, so go ahead and smile! It looks so good on you.*

I do not know whether you are religious or not, and it does not matter whether you are or are not when reading this book. When it was said that God created man in his own image, it's referring to the fact that you have a part of the source within you. You are a part of the source, regardless of whether you are religious or not. There is a part of you that is more powerful than your mind will ever be able to understand, because you mind is rational, and the rationality is based on what you have been taught, what society has told you that you are and are not.

The miracles you hear about happening all over the world are not because their God did it for them, not Buddha, or whatever the person believes in, but it is because of the light within themselves. The part inside of us all, that is a part of the source, part of the creator, part of God. Something we cannot explain, but, instead, simply experience.

WE CAN ALL CREATE MIRACLES.

But what is a miracle?

Is it something unexplained, some achievement which no one expected, or is it luck?

Here is a thought for you to ponder: could it be possible that what we call miracles is simply something slightly more than what society has programmed you to perceive as normal? In other words, could what we call miracles simple be something slightly greater than your limited beliefs?

Is anything really a miracle?

Remember when you learned something for the first time in your life, like when you learned to walk, read, write, calculate, or even when you got your first job? Before you knew how to do it, it looked like a miracle to be able to do all those things — that is to say, it was absolutely incomprehensible for you to imagine how you would ever be able to do those things. When you were able to learn those things with you mind, by repeating the activity over and over again, all those miracles became mundane. They became a part of your normal, everyday reality. There was nothing miraculous about them anymore.

Is there anything that is done over and over again that you will always call a miracle? When does it become normal? How many times does it have to be performed for you to call it normal, in your reality?

Have you allowed yourself to become so limited that something small seems big, something normal that anyone can do, you still call a miracle?

Have you caught yourself expecting less than you should or even expecting nothing, just so you will not become disappointed?

Shame on you, if you have. No, I'm just joking, you can smile, this is not so serious that we can't smile about it. Just smile, even though you might have realized something just now, something new about yourself. That you might be making yourself smaller than you really are, with less expectations than you should be having. So, for now, just throw a big smile out there at the universe, get your energy up, and think about something else.

> **From now on in your reality, from this day forward, you will not make yourself less than you are.**

You are going to keep growing and becoming more and getting to experience yourself — the real you — a little bit more today than yesterday. Remember, the real you is just in this present moment, always in the eternal now. Yesterday does not matter. The real you never judges!

The real you just wants to experience, and that's why you have this wonderful mind of yours to experience your true self in this third-dimensional world.

Now, think about your mind for a second. If your mind is the instrument chosen for the human consciousness to experience itself, then, surely, your mind must be pretty amazing. You mind is so powerful it can allow you to experience something that cannot be explained.

How have you been taking care of you mind?

Have you been treating it well?

Are you consciously stopping negative thoughts and consciously triggering positive thoughts?

Have you been taking all the tips and tricks you have learned and using them to cultivate your mind in a way that you start to reap all the beauty and wellness that you deserve in life?

YOUR MIND IS YOUR GARDEN!

You are the gardener, and everything you put in your garden grows.

What kind of seeds have you been planting in your garden?

What happens when you give negative thoughts your attention?

In other words, what happens when you sow negative thoughts in your garden — or weeds as we should call them, using this metaphor?

When you tend your garden, water it on a regular basis, and put fertilizer on it as well, feeding your mind, do you think that only the beautiful plants and seeds will benefit, or do you realize that all the bad seeds you have planted there will also benefit and grow?

Yes, of course you know that by now!

That is why you engage in exercises like stopping your negative thoughts by not giving them your attention and letting them pass through before you accidentally plant those bad seeds into the soil in your garden. Because you know that if you start to get careless and start saying something like, "Oh it's only an innocent idea, only a little seed of self-doubt, just a tiny little seed of jealousy, hatred or distress," then, you are placing those seeds into the soil, and that's where they will quietly wait until you start to water all the nice seeds in your garden. That's when you transform those little innocent bad seeds into something much worse. Those bad seeds flourish, as well as the good ones. That's why you don't plant them in your garden any more.

Which is more work: to stop planting bad seeds in your garden, or pulling the weeds later, with roots and everything?

> ***Take good care of your garden, plant beautiful, happy thoughts, and watch your garden become the most beautiful place on earth.***

Now, take some time for yourself and try to simply notice yourself in the present moment. Take a very good look at yourself by focusing on different body parts, and experience yourself in that body part in the present moment. Shift your attention slowly over your whole body as you just sit there for a few moments.

Put your attention on your left big toe!

Feel it!

Be it, and then, select a new body part to shift your attention to, and so on. Hold your attention on each part long enough to experience that body part, and see how much you can experience inside of it, in that moment. Be there, be you, and experience yourself without thought, just bring your attention completely to each body part, listen, feel, visualize and be completely in the moment and remember that you — the real you — is so wonderful in this present moment, right here and right now!

Do this now!

16

MASTER

> *You are great.*
> *You are determined, and you know what you want.*

You have taken your life, and finally, you now, allow life to happen for you, instead of life happening to you. Yes, life is happening for you. This just happened for you, because you asked for it.

You have been sending a certain frequency to the universe based on your feelings that you put behind each thought, and the universe answers by giving you more of the same.

THAT'S RIGHT, THAT JUST HAPPENED FOR YOU, BECAUSE YOU ASKED FOR IT!

You've been exceptionally good at putting yourself in the first place. You've taken a big jump in your journey of growth by taking the methods and exercises and making them your own. No one else can do it exactly like you have been doing it. You have understood the methods in your unique way, which makes it perfect because this is your journey, and there is no right nor wrong on your journey.

YOU HAVE CREATED THE ABSOLUTELY PERFECT JOURNEY.

You have also realized how much difference it makes when you read or hear something again, after your reality has been shifted, when you have grown more! You keep learning new lessons from the same books or lectures with your new perspective of life. You have learned something new each time you have read a chapter again or when reading a new chapter, and you've noticed new things in your environment, because you are and have been ready to change your current reality. You notice new things and now, you understand how your energy affects everything and everyone.

Now, you know how to raise your energy vibration and have a greater impact on the people around you than before. You are happier, you smile more, and you feel generally better, simply because you decided to. You have often over-complicated things in your life, but, now, you are not doing it as much as before. You have been doing incredibly well. You know that your journey is something you must work on all your life as long as you want to keep on growing, but, at the same time, you have arrived at the point where you also realize that it doesn't necessarily have to be all work. It can be a very fun and exciting journey of growth and play.

Now, start focusing on your current environment where you are right now.

Take a very good look around you.

Do this now!

Did you notice anything interesting?

Something new?

What do you see?

How do you feel when you look at what you just noticed?

Now, are you going to listen to your environment? In a few seconds, you will put the book down for a few seconds and just listen. Try to hear as many sounds as you can and think about what kind of sounds there are in your environment right now and where they come from. Once you've done this for a few seconds, pick the book back up.

Do this now!

Welcome back, what did you hear?

Did you hear any sounds that you did not recognize?

Did you hear any music, or did you hear something that you could not figure out where it was coming from?

By listening just now, you became totally present, by concentrating on the sounds in your current environment. Simple, yet so powerful. Well done!

Do you feel any air movement or wind on your face right now? Put your attention on the little hairs all over your face, and feel as they react or move in the wind. If there is no air movement in your environment, try to move your head around or to the sides, and create some air movement, so you can feel the air move all over your face. Worst case scenario, use your hand as a fan by moving us fast in front of you face and feel the air hit your face.

Do this now!

The small hairs work kind of like cilium, allowing you to sense all kinds of things on your skin, like the breeze for example. Now, move your attention all over your face and cup one of your palms in front of your mouth, and blow into it, as you tilt your cupped palm slightly back and forth. See if you can feel the breeze everywhere on your face.

Can you feel it under your eyes?

What about on your forehead?

What about your lips?

Cheeks?

What about in front of your right ear?

It is so amazing how you have developed the talent to be able to be totally present and concentrate on a single spot on your body and experience it. Totally focused. It's amazing how you can experience something so simple, yet so remarkable at the same time.

HOW MUCH ARE YOU WORTH?

Are you worth a lot or not?

Listen to what your gut tells you when you read this sentence out loud:

I am worth a lot!

What physical reactions did you notice as you said it out loud?

What did your gut tell you?

What did your intuition tell you?

Did you feel good as you said it? Did you get a nice sensation that spread all over your body, or did you get a knot in your stomach?

What is your body telling you about how you actually feel about yourself?

If you did get a knot in your stomach, it's something you should fix, because you are worth a lot. If that's the case, you can and should reverse the decision you made at some point in your life that you are not worth a lot. If you got a great feeling that spread all over your body, that is something I love to hear, because I know that you are worth a lot.

If you were walking outside in the wilderness, far away from any town, and you found a one-hundred-dollar bill, would you take it? Of course, you would; there is no one near you, and there is no possible way for you to find out who the original owner is. The money might have been carried by the wind many miles, for all you know. Whoever lost it could have lost it anywhere, but, now, this one-hundred-dollar bill is yours. This money is ready for a new owner.

But would you take the bill if it was very wrinkled?

Yes, of course. But what about if it was a little torn, also?

Yes, of course you would. But what about if it was also covered in mud? Would you still take it?

The answer is most likely, yes. Why are you willing to pick it up and keep it, regardless of what it looks like, wrinkled, muddy, and even torn?

Are one-hundred-dollar bills worth less if they are wrinkled?

Are they less worth a little torn or muddy?

The answer is, no, they are not. It is always worth the same number of cents if you take it to the bank, and that is why you would you pick it up: you know what it is worth.

> ***The same applies to you: no matter how wrinkled, muddy or torn apart you become, you are always worth a lot.***

Remember, no matter how you look or feel today, whatever day it is, you are always very valuable. You are worth a lot, and you are very important.

Have you ever felt that you might be worth little or nothing at all? Has the thought ever entered into your mind? If it has, I want to remind you this thought is not yours, unless you give it your attention. You have the power to allow yourself to give it no attention at all and let it pass through your mind, in and out. We all get strange thoughts from time to time, and you have learned what it takes to prevent manifesting them as your own, how to release them by ignoring them or switching to a new thought right away, by choosing your thoughts consciously. If you put your attention on a thought that you don't want to own, you are putting a bad seed into the soil in your garden.

YOU HAVE BEEN DOING A VERY NICE JOB LATELY CONSCIOUSLY PUTTING BEAUTIFUL SEEDS IN YOUR GARDEN.

You have been reading for a while now, and your progress has been absolutely amazing, just like you are. You are freaking amazing.

Sometimes, you might tend to make things harder than they really are. Sometimes, you might even think to yourself:

If I can't do this perfectly right away, I might as well not do it at all.

Does this resonate with you?

Sometimes, when you get an exceptionally great idea, it raises your energy vibration to a higher level. You feel great about the idea, and you cannot wait to share it with someone. This idea happens to be truly great, but, then, you decide to not write it down. You decide to sleep on it. You decide to put it in the back seat with Bob, and it doesn't take long before you and Bob start having a conversation about this idea in your mind. You slowly start to realize that this idea is actually not such a great idea, after all. You and Bob, have discussed the fact that most likely no one will ever want to buy it, read it, or be included in this wacky idea of yours. You finally agree with Bob — who, by the way, is always helping you stay in your comfort zone. You agree that this idea is just not that great after all, and you finally say to Bob, "Yes, you are right, my head was in the clouds. I wasn't thinking straight, this is not a good idea after all and it's going to be a hassle anyway."

Do you recognize this process? Do you relate to it?

Have you been through this process before?

Have you kept an idea to yourself long enough to rationalize it away from you or, perhaps, sold yourself the idea that you will, most likely, not be able to master the activity right away, so you might as well just forget about it?

Have you convinced yourself, inside your own mind, that the idea was not a good idea, after all?

This has most likely happened to you at some point in your life — even recently. We have all done this at some point. Let me tell you a secret that could easily change your reality completely right now. I mean, this secret could be so life-changing that you can soon start to experience all your dreams. This secret could and will, most likely, make your life more enjoyable and make you more active in fulfilling your dreams. You will become more effective, and people will start to look at you more as a role model than they already do today.

Do you want to know what this secret is?

Do I have your permission to inform you?

Go ahead, and answer yes, if you would like to know it.

THE SECRET IS THAT DONE IS YOUR NEW PERFECT.

Let me give you an example. Let's say you get an idea to write a book, for example.

Make it four times shorter than you think it should be!

Write it in less time that you think it should take to write.

Publish it with spelling errors.

Publish a brochure-sized book with spelling errors.

Yes, that is the secret that will significantly change your reality.

> *Take the next good idea, write it down, then, think for a few minutes about how you can accomplish it in the least amount of time. Then, execute it.*

You could dictate your book on your phone and, then, find someone else to type it up for you online for very little money. That would be one way you could finish your first book in a very short time. Repeat this process with your next idea, and so forth. This way, you take advantage of the creative power you were born with. You are born as a creator. But, on the other hand, you were not born a master at anything, so, now, it's time for you to stop expecting to master it before you try to create it, whatever it is.

REMEMBER THAT DONE IS YOUR NEW PERFECT.

Start to create and manifest your ideas, and don't make them perfect, just create them, because, the more you create and complete, the closer you get to becoming a master at it.

> *Rather than overcomplicating it, trying to make the right decision, make a decision, and then, make it right.*

You are getting closer to becoming a master of your personal growth journey, because you started slowly, and you have been gradually building yourself up.

Did you expect to become a master of your happiness before you started?

Did you think you would become a master of manifesting your dreams into your reality before you started to learn how to?

Exactly. You started without making any expectations that you would be a master before you started. Use that mindset towards anything you want to accomplish. Just start.

Let's take another example. You want to experience change at work, but have not have found a new job yet. You have become unmotivated at work and would really like to see some change at work.

Drive another route to work that day and get the change you crave, in small steps.

Clean up your desk or work space.

Show up in clothes you have not worn to work before or have not worn in a long time.

Make up a game, and see how many clients you can make smile or laugh today.

Turn your computer screen slightly to the left or right.

Go on your coffee break at a different time than usual.

Use another toilet at work, that you do not normally use.

Do you see how easy it is to create a small win, to create the change you crave?

YOU CAN BE HAPPY ANYWHERE WITH THE RIGHT MINDSET.

You can start creating things at home, before or after work. You could also quit your job and go do somewhere completely different. You will always become better and better at allowing yourself to act on what your intuition tells you is right for you. Create adventures in your life, and enjoy saying to yourself:

Why?

Then, take massive action!

When you get the next idea, write it down. Ask yourself, *Why do I want to do it? How can I do this quickly and get it out there?* Get it done!

> **When you keep taking action on your ideas, you are taking one step closer to becoming a master.**

One of my mentors once said to me, "Get an idea, then, sell the idea, and then, create it. That's another way of taking action right away. Doing it this way, you don't waste anytime making the perfect product and then not selling any of it. Lot of people are using this method today to create products and get them out there. Pre selling the product before it's actually been created. What a great concept.

The more small victories you can create, the more you should celebrate. Celebrate each little win on your journey. Be happy all the time; it is totally up to you, and you absolutely know that you can do it. For example, decide right now that today, you will see the beauty in everything. You're going to smile as much as you can, and you're going to allow the light inside of you to shine brightly all day.

Read these three sentences out loud:

Today, I am happy!

Today, I'm allowing my light to shine bright.

Today, I'm smiling more and allowing myself to love more than yesterday.

Now, take one hand and place it over your heart. Keep reading with your hand on your heart, and feel your heart with your hand while you keep on reading.

YOU ARE SO LUCKY!

You did not have to do anything to earn this wonderful heart of yours. It was given to you. This heart has been working for you for years without wanting anything in return. This heart was placed in you with pure love. Your heart never judges you. Your heart has unconditional love for you, and it does everything in its power to make you feel great. You own this heart; it's yours. Feel how much gratitude you have for this wonderful heart of yours, right now! Feel the sensation of gratitude as it spreads all over your body as your heart pumps gratitude throughout your veins and throughout your whole vehicle. Feel how wonderful your blood feels right now when you inhale more oxygen into your lungs and mix it with your gratitude. From there, the mix nourishes the blood, and then, your heart pumps it throughout your whole body.

Feel how it travels down to the stomach, into the thighs, down your calves and all the way down your toes and, then, back up to the heart. Now, through your hands and shoulders, then, up the neck and, finally, into your brain. Wow, what an incredible feeling to get this wonderful oxygen and gratitude in your bloodstream. Before you take your hand off your heart, think about one thing that you are really thankful for in your reality right now.

Now, allow yourself to think about everything you are grateful for and allow yourself to experience yourself in the present moment right now. Embrace your gratitude, and let go. Allow yourself to completely feel whatever comes to you. I am so grateful for you.

Be you, enjoy, and remember that the whole world is so grateful for you being you, right here and right now!

17

COLLECTIVE BELIEFS

> *Welcome back for more.*

YOU ARE FREAKING AMAZING!

You are a part of something so much greater than just you, and you realize that by now. You realize that you can receive messages from the collective consciousness, and that we are all connected. You have experienced turning off your thoughts and, then, suddenly, getting a great idea. You have managed to let go of the need to forcefully grind on and, instead, allowed yourself to trust the process and experience what you want to experience in your life, by taking the right action. Living in the present moment! Showing gratitude for events in your reality, whether it is something in the present moment or something that you know is already true in your future. You have changed your reality significantly with new ideas, a new mindset, and a new attitude towards life. You have more faith in yourself, and that is bringing you all kinds of things, opportunities, and people who have come into your reality and are now working with you, towards your dreams, directly or indirectly.

Are you still procrastinating, or have you already started to manifest all your dreams?

Have you started to write the book?

Have you already set up the orphanage?

Did you already go on that safari?

Have you finally started to paint?

Have you already started to make your dreams come true?

Take a minute to think about the dreams that you have started to manifest or have already achieved and experienced since you started reading and implementing things, ideas, processes and exercises from this book.

Is there still something stopping you?

Have you been able to unblock the limiting beliefs that have been holding you back, from your past present moments?

Have you traveled back on your timeline and changed the decision you made at some point, to limit yourself?

You can change your past decisions now, just like you can accomplish something in the future, right now! If you know what it is that has been holding you back, try this method that I am about to explain. In this example, I will use the first limiting belief I had to reverse for myself. I made a decision when I was three years old that I would have to do everything myself. That I would not have a team or people who would want to help me. I believed that I could do it better anyway, so why even bother, since I can just do it all myself. This decision was made watching my father build a new kitchen by himself, with no help at all.

You could have something similar from your past present moments. Maybe you decided that you do not deserve your dreams or that you are not worthy, because of something that happened to you as a child. It might have been watching your parents, or because of your siblings, or an incident at school. Think about what your limiting beliefs are, and then, use this method to unleash them. This is one of many methods available to break free from your limiting beliefs. Let's do this: find a pen and paper, and get comfortable in a quiet place, where you will not be interrupted, put the book down in front of you and just follow my lead.

> ***Write this down to destroy your limited beliefs. Then, you are going to talk to your subconscious mind to change what you decided to believe into what your new truth is:***

My old belief: <u>I have to do everything myself.</u>

My new true belief: <u>I am a team player, and I trust others as well as myself.</u>

THIS IS YOUR SCRIPT TO SPEAK OUT LOUD TO YOUR SUBCONSCIOUS MIND:

Hi, my subconscious mind. Up until now, we have been holding on to this old belief that <u>I have to do everything myself.</u>

I now realize that this belief is false. I want you to replace that old belief that <u>I have to do everything myself</u>, with this new true belief which is: <u>I am a team player, and I trust others as well as myself.</u>

From this day forward, I will replace the old false belief that <u>I have to do everything myself</u>, with this new true belief that <u>I am a team player, and I trust others as well as myself.</u>

I want you to a permanently replace this old false belief that <u>I have to do everything myself</u>, with this new, true belief that <u>I am a team player, and I trust others as well as myself</u>, permanently. Make it so now and forever!

Then, you repeat this last statement for five, ten, twenty minutes, or however long it will take to release your block. You will feel it when this is done, when you transform the vibration of your subconscious mind, there will be no doubt: you will feel it, you will know when it is done.

Do this now!

Now that this is done, don't forget to thank your subconscious mind, like you would thank an old friend for good advice or how you would thank someone who wants to invest in you or someone who has just given you a priceless gift.

If, for any reason, the old belief surfaces in the next two weeks, be alert, and catch it right when it surfaces, and say this out loud, and laugh at it. No, I don't believe that anymore. Now, I have this new true belief that <u>I am a team player, and I trust others as well as myself.</u> This will shift your vibration back into alignment right then and there.

Well done! How do you feel right now? Did you feel the shift when it happened? Wasn't it magical?

Just in case you thought about not doing the exercise, stop right now, and do it. Do not continue any further, until you have experienced the magic. If you cannot do this now for whatever reason, then close the book right here, and come back to it when you can.

Do you know what you fear?

If you have not started to make your dreams come true, what's stopping you? Maybe you are just about to start? There is no reason why you should not be well on your way manifesting your dreams, after reading all the previous chapters and implementing the exercises like you have been doing. Maybe you did not do the exercises, and that would explain why you have not started your journey by now. But I will allow myself to doubt that. I do not think you would be this far into this book without seeing for yourself the magic that happens in your reality by implementing the strategies and easy exercises.

If you have been doing all the exercises and yet, you are not on your way towards your dreams, or, for whatever reason, you decided not to do the exercises at all, then, you might just need a boost to start your journey now!

You can contact me personally to see if we are a fit. If I can become your personal coach, I, or someone on my team, will hold you accountable. You can also pick the coach or mentor you prefer on your own — it's totally up to you. If you have not yet started to work on your dreams in any way by now, it is time for you to say this out loud:

I am ready.

Listen to your intuition, and select a coach who has done what you dream of performing. If you're already busy making your dreams come true and taking daily action already, you can achieve them more quickly by getting a coach or mentor. Those who have already done what you want to achieve can tell you what to avoid and what to do. Almost everyone who achieves great success in life had and still has a coach or a mentor to guide him or her. Even super-successful people have someone who they can get feedback from on questions that come up, or get feedback on their current plans, contracts, and ideas. You can achieve so much more with someone who stands firmly behind you and someone who backs you up with a different point of view.

> *A smart person learns from their mistakes. A wise person learns from other people's mistakes and successes.*

Do you believe in yourself by now?

Do you believe that you can do it?

At first, you start to believe that you can, and then, when your faith in yourself becomes strong enough, you start to know for a fact that you can.

There is a big difference between believing you can and knowing you can.

When you believe, you can do anything you can think of.

WHEN YOU KNOW YOU CAN, YOU CAN NO LONGER FAIL.

Let's suppose you want to go from your house to the store, and you are absolutely sure you can do it. You know you can, even though you do not have access to a car, you do not have a bike, and it's too far to walk. Still, you know for a fact that you will be able to get there, and because you are 100 percent sure, you turn your head and see the solution. You can take a taxi, take the bus, hitchhike, or call a friend or family member who can give you a lift. When you are absolutely sure about it, you do not need to know how; it's enough to know that you can, because the solution will be revealed to you. The reason for that is that you are taking action, and you have your eyes open looking for the how. You are so sure about it, and you know you cannot fail, even if the impossible happens. Let's say that the store vanishes into a sinkhole. That does not change the fact that you will be able to get to the store to get what you need from the store; this only changes your destination, not the outcome! Because, now, you will simply go to another store. The same applies to any dreams you are manifesting. Once you know for a fact that it will happen, you do not need to know how. On your way there, the destination might change slightly, but you will experience your dreams, and that is a known fact, my friend. You will manifest it into your reality. You will make it happen. This might be something you've never done before, but when you know for a fact you can do it, the answer can come from anywhere. From your coach, mentor or family member, for example.

Not seeing something does not mean that it does not exist. What has often stopped you is what you do not know or have not seen. When the sun is blocked by clouds, it's still there, and just like this metaphor, your answers often reveal themselves when you remove the clouds. You may also be blinded by what society has programmed you to think you can and cannot do. Today, you have opened up your mind, and if, for any reason, you do not believe or do not know yet that you can do anything, you should, at least, be very close to it. You would definitely get more confident with coaching, that's a fact. You would take more action and learn how you can do things with less effort and become more productive and efficient.

ARE YOU ALREADY TAKING ACTION TO MAKE YOUR DREAMS COME TRUE?

Now, imagine yourself, in your future, and it's your last day here on earth, and you are like you will become, if you continue without chasing your dreams. You meet another version of yourself. You are meeting the version of you that started today, taking action and striving toward making all your dreams come true and to becoming the best version of yourself every single day.

Take a few seconds to visualize this scenario.

WHICH VERSION DO YOU WANT TO BECOME?

How coachable are you?

Do you know what that means?

That means how good are you at emptying your glass to make room for new ideas and processes, to learn something new?

How good are you in accepting a new truth?

How good are you at taking advice, accepting it, and implementing it?

Can you be coached to live a better life?

Can you be coached to make your dreams come true?

Do you want to make your dreams come true, or have you already given up?

Did you know that Colonel Sanders failed to put KFC on the map until he was 62 years old?

> *You cannot let anyone tell you what you cannot do. Then, you are no longer controlling your reality, and therefore, you are no longer taking responsibility for your reality.*

Are you doing something today that is just because, or because it has always been done that way?

Do you have any traditions that you do, but do not know why you do it or where it came from?

There was a family in Iceland who made the best rack of lamb in the world on Christmas Eve! They used ropes to constrict the rack of lamb tightly together, and it took a lot of effort to prepare it such a way, but without exception, the rack was absolutely amazing. A young girl in the family asked after several generations of this tradition, why it was done that way, and no one knew why. Thankfully, her great-grandmother was still alive at the time, and she told the girl that her great-grandmother always used to tie down the rack of lamb, because it was the only way to fit it into the small oven at the time. Her oven was simply too small for the rack of lamb, and therefore, she had to constrict the size of the rack with ropes to fit it in the small oven. Yet, everyone in the family was absolutely 100 percent sure that with this tradition, the rack of lamb would taste awesome, if not become the best tasting rack of lamb in the world. That's exactly what the family experienced each time over the holidays.

Do you have something in your reality today that you always do, but you do not know why?

This example about the rack of lamb teaches us two things! Sometimes, we do things, yet, we do not know why we are doing them, and the other lesson is that if enough people are sharing a collective belief, it can become their truth. Their expectations, energy, and beliefs create a unified reality.

Social behavior is something that is interesting to think about. Let me tell you about one study that was done on monkeys. Five monkeys were placed in a cage with a ladder in the middle, and at the top of the ladder, the researchers hung a bunch of bananas.

When the monkeys went to climb the ladder, the researchers gave all five monkeys an electric shock. Shortly thereafter, all the monkeys stopped trying to climb the ladder. When the monkeys stopped trying, they took one monkey from the cage and put a new monkey into the cage, who did not know the social rules or the consequences. He immediately went to the ladder, and when he did, the other four monkeys attacked the new monkey and started to beat him up — understandably, because they did not want to be electrocuted for his naive behavior. Shortly thereafter, no one was trying to climb the ladder. Then, they took one of the four original monkeys out and put a new monkey into cage. History repeated itself; even the monkey that had not experienced the electrocution participated in beating this new monkey up for the mistake of trying to climb the ladder. They kept replacing the original monkeys, one at a time, until none of the monkeys in the cage knew about the electric shock. However, all the monkeys continued to attack the new monkey if he tried to climb the ladder. The new monkey learned very quickly what the social norm was in that cage!

I don't know why, but if someone tries to climb the ladder, we beat him up!

How many things do you think we do in our society today because it's always been like that, or just because? For example, many people are selling themselves the idea that they can't do something, because their family has never been able to do it before, or even worse, perhaps selling themselves the idea that they can't do something because someone told them so. If enough people believe you cannot do something, it might come true. That is to say, if you participate in that belief.

How many must believe in something, so that it will become their truth?

What is a collective belief, anyway?

Money is a very good example. There are enough people who believe in money, and that is why money has value. In the United States, money was once backed up by gold, but since 1971, the U.S. dollar is a currency that is based on the faith people have in it.

What about a business: is it real, or does a business only exist, because enough people believe that it exists?

Let's say you go and start a business, you pay the fees, and suddenly, you own your own brand-new company, on a piece of paper.

But how was it really created?

What if a judge makes a judgment and declares your business bankrupt or if the law changes all of a sudden?

There might be a possibility that your company will no longer exist.

Did it ever exist, or was it only perceived as real, while enough people still believed it was real?

What about food? How many have to believe that a specific food is unhealthy, so that it will have a negative impact on your body?

The government and people in control will often manipulate the news to create a religion, a cult, or a limited belief for people, so that it will be easier to control them. Thankfully, there is always someone who refuses to believe that, which no one knows why they should believe in the first place and manages to prove that it is possible to do things in a different and better way.

In the year 1983, the 61-year-old Australian Cliff Young ran for the first time in the ultra-marathon. He did not look at what other people had done on this 875-kilometer-long run (about 544 miles), and by him not knowing what the social norm was in the race, he showed up in his farmer boots and won the race. Not only did he win the race, but he shattered the old record by almost two days.

What he did not know is that everyone who ran this long race went to sleep at night and ran during the daytime. Because he did not know that, he ran for five days, fifteen hours, and four minutes, without stopping. He was dead last after the first day, but took the lead during the first night while others slept.

How many people do you think slept in this race after 1983?

That's right, no one, because he showed them that this was possible. His record was beat the following year. Nevertheless, he was and remains a hero to this day for this accomplishment.

It's not always a good idea to blindly do what others are doing. Sometimes, you must evaluate for yourself how things are done, instead of just doing exactly as others have been doing.

> **When you have a coach, it's up to you to evaluate his advice and then, listen to your intuition and make the best possible decision, based on your own intuition, and then, take action.**

The entrepreneur Steve Jobs, the founder of Apple, said that what is important in life is to connect the dots to see the whole picture. Not by trying to connect the points into the future, but afterward. Then, you can see the big picture that the universe is painting for you. As he said himself, in 1985, he had lost the company Apple away from him, and at that point, he had to decide either to go into great depression and give up, or simply start over. It was a difficult time for him, and it took him about six months to start over. In the years away from Apple, he founded NeXT, and he also bought Pixar, which he turned into a global brand with his vision and leadership. The technology in NeXT later became the core of Apple, after Apple bought NeXT. Pixar became the biggest animation company in the world. In 1997, Steve was rehired by Apple, and he took the company from near-failure into the superpower and status symbol that it is today. He did not see it until afterward, that when he was fired from Apple, that was the best thing that could have ever happened to him in his life.

> *We all go through tough times, and we all hit walls at some point or have some sort of relapse. Just remember, it might be exactly what's best for your journey, but you might not see it until later.*

Now, place your attention on your breath, and pay attention to how you are breathing. Put your index finger and middle finger on your throat, and feel your heart beating.

Is your heart beating fast or slowly?

Do this now!

Nice work. Now, put your attention back on your breathing. Now, try to breathe in reverse! When you breathe out, put your stomach out, and when you breathe in, pull your stomach in. Try this for a minute now, and feel how this affects your entire body.

Do this now!

Your brain has two parts, the right and left hemisphere. Now, we are going to synchronize them together. Put both hands out in front of you, at shoulder height straight forward. With your left hand, create the letter L in the air, with your hand extended straight out in front of you, keep repeating it up and down and then, at the same time, use your right hand to create a circle in the air and keep that hand straight as well. Pay close attention to what's happening in your mind and body when you do this. How much attention do you need to accomplish this?

Try this now!

Did you accomplish this?

Great, now change it up. Make a circle with your left hand and the letter L with your right hand.

Do that now!

Excellent job! When you do this easy exercise for three to five minutes, you synchronize your hemispheres, and if you read something immediately afterward, you remember it a whole lot better. You have a better memory and learn more quickly after such an easy exercise. There are so many great things happening for you when you do a simple exercise like that. For example, it reduces depression, anxiety, worry, and more. It increases attention, memory and your intelligence, to name a few.

Feel free to use this exercise before learning anything new or when you need to calm your mind. You can also accomplish the same thing with your feet to synchronize your hemispheres. It also has the same effect on your brain when you practice juggling three balls between your hands.

YOU ARE FREAKING AWESOME!

Now, use the time to just be here and enjoy how wonderful you are. Sit here for a minute and enjoy experiencing how ready you are to take action and make your dreams come true, right here and right now!

18

MEMORY

> *You are incredible. It is quite an achievement to come back for more, for as many times as you have done now and keep reading more stuff that motivates and inspires you to look within. You are beautiful.*

Do you realize how much impact your simple choices have on your journey, like wanting to read more and then, actually doing it? You should be proud: you are doing so much more than the average person is doing today. Often, what separates those who live and enjoy life and those who do not, is just the matter of doing it, taking the initiative. Taking action, just like you have been doing, repeatedly, and are doing right now.

That's often the only difference between success and not. Taking action, one step at a time. When you empower yourself, when you strengthen you will and go for it, you feel better, and you know that all so well by now, but it is not enough to just know it. There are a lot of people who know what is good for them, but they simply just don't do it.

> *You are so freaking amazing on your journey of growth, taking action again and again.*

Often, we really mean to do things, but we just forget to do them, right?

Why do we forget to do some of the things we know are good for us?

Perhaps, your memory is not that good. Maybe, you did not get good memory genes?

You might have heard things like, "Wow, her memory is really good," or, "He got his memory from his father."

Do I have your permission to tell you something amazing now that could potentially change your reality once again? You can answer yes, now with your inner voice or out loud.

It's amazing to get opportunities in life to learn new things that shift your reality. To learn something we assumed was true, and then, BOOM, you either accept a new truth and shift your reality, or you simply discard it and carry on with the reality you have created for yourself.

So, here we go! Did you know that your memory is only one-third genetics? That leaves two-thirds that you can improve by learning how and practicing.

Isn't that great news?

Anyone can learn to remember incredible things. In this chapter, we are going to touch the surface of some of the methods you can use to help you remember more.

Would you like to learn to remember more?

Yes, of course, we all benefit from having better memory.

Before we go into the topic of increasing your memory, here is an exercise you do for the next seven days. If you have done this exercise before, you only need to do it for two days now, to sharpen the edge of your blade, so to speak. It's so important to keep your mind positive, and part of that process is to allow your thoughts to come in and go back out, depending on whether that thought serves you or not. Everything you give your attention to grows and gets magnified. When you get a thought that you do not want grow and manifest, take notice to the fact that this thought is not yours, and instead of putting your attention on that thought, put your attention immediately to counting the unwanted thoughts you do not want, the negative thoughts or thoughts patterns that make you feel bad. For the next seven days, notice each thought you don't want to plant in your garden, and write down the count on a piece of paper — or use your phone — every time you have a negative thought that comes for a visit. By shifting your attention to counting them, you allow them to pass through. Focusing on counting and not the thought itself. The thought floats back out while you note it down on paper or your phone that another unwanted visit happened that you did not appreciate. It doesn't really matter how you count them — with letters, numbers, words, sentences, or any other way you choose to count them. You just need to do it, and just watch how you improve on not receiving negative thoughts once your attention gets used to counting them and not focusing on them. Shifting your thoughts to something else, something beautiful. Slowly but surely, less and less unwanted thoughts that don't serve you appear, by having an alert attention and intention on counting them and letting them pass through. Then, you can place your attention on the beautiful thoughts that appear and make your life better and more beautiful. If you have never done it before, do this for the next seven days. If this is not your first rodeo, then only do it for two days this time.

It's inspiring how you have been taking all the exercises and making them your own. Owning them and executing them, knowing that the more you repeat the exercises, the better your life will become, and the happier you will become slowly but surely, one step at a time. You must remember to write it down as you count the negative thoughts appearing for the next few days, because it will not work, unless you do the work. If you need a reminder, create a few alarms on your phone as a reminder throughout the day, reminding you to write it down as you count the thoughts you don't want to give a permanent address in your garden.

Before smartphones, we did not have this convenient method of storing phone numbers like we do now, so we had to memorize the numbers we used most frequently. It was common to know anywhere from 10 to 20 phone numbers without a problem, even more. Today, we rely heavily on the smartphone, or computers, or cloud storage. We do not need to remember anything, really. We can just look it up on our phone or computer, no matter what it is. It's rare to remember many phone numbers today, because we don't need to.

How's your memory when you meet a person face to face for the first time? Can you always remember their names?

Did you know that you could remember phone numbers, credit card numbers, passport numbers, and names of all the people you get to know, if you wanted to?

There is a method to get better at remembering that enables us to be able to do just that. It is a method that is not taught in schools, at least not as far as I know.

Now, you are going to learn a few things that are going to benefit your memory, and if you ever have to teach anyone else how to enhance their memory, you are going to learn how to do that, as well.

Are you ready to become an even better version of yourself right now?

Great. In remembering anything, there is a rule of thumb: the more you can use as many of your senses, the better it will work for you. That is to say, putting things in perspective, or by telling a story and experiencing the story with as many of your senses as possible to make it easier to recall any facts, names, or numbers.

Let's start off with a very simple example.

You have nine cards, and all the cards have a picture of something different on them. You're going to teach a five-year-old child to remember all nine cards. You turn all the cards up in a three-by-three box, so that the child can see the cards. The pictures on the cards are in this order:

Monkey	Dancing lady	Glass of water
Umbrella	Cloud	Dog
Tall building	Milkshake	Phone

Now, you allow the child to look over the cards for a minute and then, turn them back over, so the pictures are facing down now. Wait another 30 seconds before you ask the child to tell you what is on each card as you turn them back around in the same order. The child will try hard to get these right! Perhaps, if the child is very gifted, he or she will guess the majority right, but most likely not. The child will most likely be able to correctly guess anywhere from two to five cards, but, of course, there are exceptions.

Now, you are going to teach another child to remember all the cards, with the story approach. You put the same cards down on the table, in the same order, in front of this other child, who has not seen these cards before. Then, as you turn each one of the cards up, say:

This monkey loves to dance. One day, he was dancing with this dancing lady, and when they had danced for a little while, the monkey was so thirsty he reached for a glass of water, and he drank it so fast that a lot of the water spilled out of his mouth. Thankfully, the dancing lady reached out and grabbed an umbrella to protect her dress from the spewing water. Then, a gust of wind swiped the umbrella out of her hand and into the clouds. As the umbrella floated into the sky around the clouds, a flying dog came by and saw the umbrella floating there. He looked surprised. This was a superdog with a cape, flying around the clouds looking to see if someone needed his help. Then, he heard screaming coming from a tall building close by, so he flew in to see what was wrong. On the tall building, he saw a man holding his head screaming, because he had been drinking a milkshake too fast and had a brain freeze. The dog was so happy to see that there was nothing seriously wrong that he picked up his smartphone and took a selfie with the man, laughing at the whole thing.

Now, you turn the card back over and wait 30 seconds before you start, before the child begins to guess. Then, you encourage the child to start repeating your story again, you point to the back of the first card and encourage your child to take part of the story, by asking, for example, who loved to dance? Once you've done this two or three times, with a new set of nine cards each time, then, you teach your child to create their own story and remember all the cards that way. I did this with my daughter when she was five years old, and I can confirm that this method works. Now, please try it out yourself to find out for yourself how effective this method really is. There is nothing like experiencing this yourself.

This is a very easy, powerful way to remember, and now, we are going to test this approach with a different subject, for adults.

Are you ready?

Read this story, and see how much you will remember after reading it:

A one-dollar bill with George Washington was shared by two friends, John Adams and Thomas Jefferson, who both signed their names on the dollar bill, which was later known as the Declaration of Independence. Sadly, a few years later, James the Outlaw and his Four Mad Sons watched the British Army burn down the White House with the dollar bill inside of it. The steam that came from the fire was used for the first steamboat ride, which president James, who did not like to row, rode on, and as he was giving everyone on board high fives, the boat hit an iceberg. As the boat was sinking, they saw a John Doe, quenching his thirst in the river before 6 a.m. that morning. He was swimming butt naked, like Adam and Eve. A Jew was standing on shore, watching the whole thing, jacked up on 7UP while his sons tried to pull him to the train station. On their way to the train station, they saw eight unprotected martinis sitting on top of a van that was buried halfway down into the ground. Then, William the Protector arrived at the van with a hen which was reaching for his wallet. Everyone was shocked to see him start harassing the hen. They called to William (the Protector), "Why are you doing this?" He replied he was sorry, it was an accident. As he said it, he fell down and ripped his coat. Oh no, now, I need an anonymous John Doe to Tyler my tenth coat.

This was a bit weird story, don't you think? You probably know already what this story was teaching you to remember, right? That's right, the full name of the first ten presidents of the United States in the right order. When we have a story to remember something, it is important that we can visualize the story as we hear it, read it, and/or tell it. This can be done with anything. Let's take a quick look at how this story works and why I chose those words in the story.

A one-dollar bill with George Washington was shared by two friends, John Adams and Thomas Jefferson, who both signed their names on the dollar bill, which was later known as the Declaration of Independence.

The first president was George Washington, and most people associate him with the one-dollar bill, and that's perfect for the first president. John Adams and Thomas Jefferson were presidents two and three, and they were the only two presidents to sign the Declaration of Independence. They were very close friends and very connected to each other. They even died on the same day.

Sadly, a few years later, James the Outlaw and his Four Mad Sons watched the British Army burn down the White House with the dollar bill inside of it.

Outlaw James is referring to Jesse James, just as a reference, because the fourth president was James Madison, hence, the Outlaw James with his Four Mad Sons. The British did invade and burn the White House during his time in office.

The steam that came from the fire was used for the first steamboat ride, which president James, who did not like to row, rode on, and as he was giving everyone on board high fives, the boat hit an iceberg.

High fives because he was the fifth president, and he was the first president to ride a steamboat ride. His name was James Monroe, or James who did not like to roe.

As the boat was sinking, they saw a John Doe Quenching his thirst in the river before 6 a.m. that morning. He was swimming butt naked, like Adam and Eve.

Before 6 a.m., because it's the 6th president, but also because John Quincy Adams did swim naked every early each morning, and there is a story around how a female reporter stole his clothes during his naked morning swim and held the clothes hostage until he agreed to be interviewed. That's a first time a president of the United States was interviewed by a female.

A Jew was standing on shore, watching the whole thing, Jacked up on 7UP while his Sons tried to pull him to the train station.

The 7th president was Andrew Jackson, A Jew, like Andrew, and he was jacked up on 7UP, and his sons were pulling him to the train station. Jacked up plus sons make Jackson, and he was the first president to ride on a presidential train ride.

On their way to the train station, they saw eight unprotected Martinis sitting on top of a Van that was Buried halfway down into the ground.

Eighth president, so eight unprotected martinis, his name was Martin Van Buren, the Van was halfway Buried into the ground. We use unprotected to set up the next name, which is William, and it means a protector.

Then, William the Protector arrived at the van with a hen reaching for his wallet. Everyone was shocked to see him start harassing the hen.

The ninth president was William Henry Harrison, so William had a hen reaching for his wallet. Then, he started harassing the hen.

They called to William (the Protector), "Why are you doing this?" He replied he was sorry, it was an accident. As he said it, he fell down and ripped his coat. Oh no, now, I need an anonymous John Doe to Tyler my tenth coat.

The tenth president was John Tyler.

Do you see how picturesque the story becomes?

How easy it is to visualize it, as it's being told or read?

The more the story gets weird and vivid, the better it will work. It does not have to be rude or hateful, but often what shakes us up or catches us off guard, is what sticks best to our long-term memory. Perhaps, you already knew the full names of the first ten presidents of the United States before you heard this story, but if not, it is very likely that you can recall this story to remember all ten presidents of the United States, their full names, and in the right sequence. But if you want to be able to never forget it, you need to repeat the story 14 times over the next 28 days. Then, you will never forget it. That's a promise!

The story method can be used to remember anything. Now, let's try something else. Let's try to remember some numbers. You will read these 14 numbers, and then, you will close the book and try to write them down on a piece of paper. Only read them once through. Are you ready?

$$1-9-4-4-8-0-7-0-2-1-2-0-1-8.$$

Now, close the book and write them on a piece of paper and see how many you get right.

How did you do in remembering these 14 numbers?

Most people can remember four to eight numbers, and it's perfectly normal if you did not get all the numbers in your first attempt. We will try again with the same numbers, but, now, I'll teach you how you can put the numbers together to remember them. Let's try this again, with a better way to remember them, here are these 14 numbers again:

$$1944 - 80 - 70 - 21 \text{ and } 2018.$$

Now, close the book and try again.

How did you do this time around? Better, right?

Did you recall all 14 numbers now? 1944, 80, 70, 21, and 2018. It is likely that you caught them all this time.

Well done. Now, you have learned how to reorganize the information you want to remember, and when you put them in story or in a pile, it becomes so much easier to remember them.

You could even put the numbers into the story method to remember them even better. For example, you could say that in 1944, 80 men and 70 women playing 21 or blackjack, as it's called. This is the only official tournament that is known to have turned into an orgy, but it was not until 2018 that we found the journal of one of the women, and in it, we can read that all the women that night were actually lady-boys. Lol, this is not a true story, just saying.

It's only put this way to demonstrate the power of shocking the listener. Yes, you. You will be more likely to remember the facts if it throws you off your norm. Of course, we do not recommend making up lies, but if you can find true, relevant facts that can be presented in a shocking way, then go for it. You can also create a fantasy type of story where the listener is not being lied to, because he get's that it's a story.

YOU ARE FREAKING AMAZING, YOU KNOW THAT RIGHT?

Your progress and growth so far, is absolutely phenomenal, almost superhero-like. For example, you are now starting to comprehend that your memory can be so much better than you even imagined, just by using better methods of remembering things that you want to remember. Now that you realize that two-thirds of your memory is exercise and methodology, it's going to have a very positive impact on your reality.

The next time you meet a new person, you can use these methods to remember their name, for example. The first thing to remember, when meeting people, is to always repeat their name out loud after you hear their name. For example, you might say something like this, "Jennifer, that's a beautiful name. It reminds me of my favorite actor." Of course, that is just an example. By connecting the name to something true in your reality, you remember that this woman you just met reminds you of your favorite actor, but if the connection is to something that is not flattering or positive, then, of course, you will not say that part out loud.

To become great at this memory game, you must practice it over and over again, just like with everything else in your reality that you want to become a master at. Repeat the exercise until you never forget a name again, and when you do, it will do wonders for you career, whatever your career is, because there is nothing that people like to hear more than their own name, in most cases anyway. It makes us all feel important when people remember our name.

Just repeat their name, and connect it to something you notice the first time you meet that person. Maybe the person is tall, and you can connect their name to their height, or maybe they speak loudly, or maybe you met that person at a bar and saw her dropping a few pennies from her purse, and her name is Penny. Then, you can connect her name to the pennies you saw falling from her purse. Those examples you would, of course, not want to say out loud, unless we can do it in a positive or flattering manner. There are endless possibilities for you to connect any name, so that you remember it, always. The more you practice, the faster and better you will be at it. You could assign a person's name to a song or some facts in lyrics from one of your favorite songs, and you could sing it with your inner voice as you meet that person to remember the name.

Now, it's time for you to start practicing and see what method works best for you to remember names. You have an unlimited power source inside of you, and what you might have thought of as talents or genetics before, you now know is often nothing more than practice and methodology.

REMEMBER THAT YOU ARE ABSOLUTELY AMAZING AND UNLIMITED.

Now, put the book down in front of you and keep reading. Put your palms together in front of your heart, and start to rub them together to create energy. Do it as if you were trying to keep your hands warm. Rub them together until you begin to feel how they start getting warmer and warmer.

Just like that, yes. Even a little more pressure and then, you produce more energy.

Yes, just like that, fantastic job.

Now, take your positively charged hands, and place them both over your heart and read this out loud:

I am so grateful for this heart of mine.

I'm so lucky I did not have to do anything to earn this heart filled with unconditional love.

Well done, that was amazing!

Now, you can pick the book up again!

Amazing how you just raised your energy vibration with gratitude, just now.

Don't you feel great right now?

YOU MUST BE FEELING GREAT RIGHT NOW. THAT WAS AMAZING! YOU ARE AMAZING!

Now, try to recall the story about the first ten presidents of the United States. Practice repeating the story about the one-dollar bill owned by his two friends, John and Thomas, who signed the bill, which was later burned down with the White House and James and his Four Mad Sons watched it burn.

After you try that, remember to start counting the number of negative thoughts you will let pass in and out for the next seven days.

Enjoy feeling how truly amazing and unlimited you are, right here and right now.

19

WITNESS

> *You are back, well done.*
> *You are staying active, and you are absolutely freaking awesome.*

The reason you keep coming back for more is that you are starting to experience more and more of what you deserve in life, more joy, and more experiences. But not all experiences are pleasant. Sometimes, you experience something you do not enjoy at all.

How are those experiences affecting you today?

Have you reached a point where you enjoy experiencing everything life has to offer?

Can you allow yourself to experience the good and the bad without resistance?

Can you completely let go and experience the sadness in the same way you experience joy?

Do you know how important it is to be able to let go, in order to not block your flow of life energy?

This applies to both good experiences and the bad. That's why it is so important to be completely in the present moment during the experience and allow the experience to come in and back out, once it is time. Allowing the flow of energy to pass through your chakras (your energy points) and not hanging on to it and clogging the flow of your life force. This flow of energy, that flows through you, every day, is often call chi, life force, prana, or spirit. The greater the flow of your life energy is, the better your life will be in every way.

It's a similar principle to your thoughts that you do not want to put your attention on. You allow your experience to come in as easily as you allow them to go back out. If you hang onto your experiences, it's like giving negative thoughts your attention. You plant bad seeds in your garden. Hanging on to your experiences will clog the flow of energy, and you don't want that. Your flow of energy is fundamental for your spiritual growth, and also important for your body to heal itself. Energy clogs or blocks can cause you self-sabotage later on, once you have accomplished something. When old emotional patterns resurface, you relive the experience, and that's why it is so important to allow the energy to flow through, always. In yoga, this is known as samskaras, which are emotional energy patterns that we hold on to in response to events that we experience, that can resurface as an emotional response to certain situations later on.

Next time you feel something uncomfortable coming to the surface — an old emotional pattern resurfacing — use that as an opportunity to release it right then.

Take a deep breath, and when you let the air powerfully back out, just say:

I release this, or *I will not hold on to this anymore.*

Then, count backwards from five. Five, four, three, two, one, and then, focus on something else or choose another thought right away. It is not really that difficult, but this is just like everything else: you need to practice this process over and over again before you can master it. With practice and time, you can become a master of releasing your energy blocks, which, most of the time, are located in your heart center.

Try this the next time an unpleasant sensation resurfaces: take a deep breath, blow it out, count backwards from five, and drop the feeling. This simple process will change a lot of things for you. You will accomplish this with a breeze, because you're freaking amazing.

> **Decide right now with your intentions that you will no longer block your flow of energy, and your subconscious mind will support you with that decision.**

When you are outside walking, are you speaking to yourself?

Is your inner voice talking about something that does not matter?

Is it distracting you?

Did I forgot to turn off the TV?

Did I forget to lock the front door?

How long is this walk?

I have to remember to take the book back to work tomorrow!

Are you listening to your inner voice?

Most of us do it all the time. This voice always has something to say. It tries it best to keep you in the comfort zone. This voice also has a way of spotting a potential problem with a project or identify flaws that other people seem to have.

You and this voice are close friends, right? This voice is your mind speaking to you. Imagine if you would start saying everything that your inner voice is telling you every day. Do you think you would be the guest of honor at parties blurring out stuff like:

Wow, you've really put on a lot of weight since the last time I saw you.

or

Wow, I barely recognized her. She is aging really fast now.

On the other hand, this voice also has some nice things to say. It's unbelievable, when you think about it, what we are saying to ourselves every single day. Now, imagine if you could take this voice of yours out of your body and put it into another body, and now, you're going to spend all your time with this person, forever.

How long do you think it would take for you to get fed up with the constant chattering, good and bad, every day, all day?

Exactly, yet, at the same time, you do not think it's a big deal that you do spend all day with that person inside your head every day, and you keep on listening to all the crap this voice has to say, all day long.

This voice is not you. You are the witness, you are the one who sees what the body sees, hears what the mind is saying, and so on. You are pure attention, awareness or consciousness. You are using this body of yours to experience this life here on earth.

Without thought, what is there?

Pure awareness, yes, but what is there without awareness?

One of the fundamental questions you can ask yourself is, who am I?

Then, answer it.

Who are you?

You might want to say something like, "I am a woman," "I am a man," "I am a teacher," "I am a driver," "I am married," "I am this or that," trying to explain yourself as something tangible.

But is that right?

Is that you?

You are so much more than that. Ask again, who am I? Continue to ask yourself that question again and again. Who sees what your eyes see?

Who is it that feels what your body feels?

Who are you?

You can ask yourself this question many times a day. Some say that this is the only question that matters, but that is, of course, entirely up to you to find out yourself by asking this question.

Who am I, that is experiencing all of this?

Who am I?

Have you seen the movie *The Terminator*, starring Arnold Schwarzenegger?

If not, don't worry. In short, the movie is about an artificial intelligence computer system that tries to eliminate the human race. They create a supercomputer to oversee the defense system of the United States, and when the system, Skynet, went live, it only took a few days for the system to become self-aware. The computer realizes that it was learning, becoming aware of it self. It became the witness behind the learning. When Skynet became self-aware, it determined that the biggest threat to earth was the human race. So, it decided to eliminate the human race. Of course, this is only a movie, but, nevertheless, it's is a very relevant metaphor for this chapter as to what happens in real life when you become self-aware.

> *Becoming self-aware is when you realize that you are the witness or awareness behind your thoughts, your emotions, and your experiences. That moment is called becoming self-aware.*

Have you noticed when your awareness sometimes goes outside your body?

For example, when you're watching a movie or something else that captivates your entire attention. You are in Alpha state, when you are completely focused on anything. When you are completely in the movie or whatever you are watching or doing. Just for a second, imagine that you could go and watch a movie that would consume all your senses: smell, hearing, sight, taste, and touch. Who are you at that moment, when all your tools to experience are overtaken by something other than your body or inner voice. Who are you then?

We are all seeking something. It could be something you have been programmed to think you should be seeking, but hopefully you are seeking the truth outside your social programming. You might have a dream to build your own house. We all have goals, large or small, but what happens when you reach your goals, and you have not set a new goal by then?

Do you know happens then?

Do you know what happens when you take that deep breath of satisfaction after reaching that goal, without a new goal or dream and what happens when you say to yourself:

Oh, Yeah, I did it. That's it? I am done?

That's the second you stop growing and stop enjoying your life like you should, but, of course, this does not happen all at once, that very second, but that is the moment you shift your vibration and start shrinking. Then, your inner voice — Bob — starts to reason why you should stay in the comfort zone, in the known. He tries and tries again to make you believe that now, you should just sit back in the leather recliner, kick back, and start to relax! That's it. You are done, you did it.

Let's pretend for a minute that you were really poor when you grew up, and you lived in a house where the roof leaked water, and you always dreamed of living in better house than you were brought up in. When you were old enough, you started to work and save money to be able to build your dream house. This project takes a long time, and one day, you finally have the foundation ready. Gradually, the walls are built, and so on. Then, about 20 years later, you have completed your perfect house. It's ready. Your house is absolutely perfect. It's so perfect, you don't need anything outside your house to thrive right now. You are so happy there. Time starts passing by without new goals or growth, while you stay cozy, curled up inside your new home. Now, thoughts start to sneak in, that someone might want to break into the house and steal or damage something in your perfect house. It does not take long before you have turned your house into a fortress. That is to say, you have barred up the doors and windows, so no one can enter the house. The next step is fear creeping in about the possibility that people outside the house might want to harm you, so you decide to never go out again, and why should you, the house is perfect. This fear keeps growing, and you start to completely avoid people. You stop paying the electric bill, because you are no longer working and have no cash flow, and very soon, you are all alone in this prison you call a home, with a candle as your only light, and you are running out of food. Now, you must overcome this enormous fear you have created within yourself, simply to survive.

This is exactly what is happening every day to so many people in real life. You are afraid to speak in front of a crowd, or to create the company that you wanted so bad to start a long time ago, or you are too afraid to move abroad. This happens gradually over time. Slowly but surely, your dreams become smaller, one at a time. Some call this progress, growing up, but me, I call it listening to Bob. What's dreams are hidden inside your fortress? In your cemetery of dreams, how many dreams are buried there alive? That's right they are still alive even thought you might have thought otherwise after burying them.

What is it that you have convinced yourself that you cannot do today, but at some point in time, back in your past, you knew you could and wanted to do?

Have you ever seen one of those electronic dog collars? Pins in the ground with sensors create a radius that the dog should not go beyond. When the dog gets close to the pins, the collar starts to vibrate, and if the dogs keeps going anyway, the dog will get an electric shock. This electric shock is not life-threatening, but it's very uncomfortable; it hurts. If the dog is very assertive, he can get through it. First, the collar starts to vibrate, and then, the electrocution starts, but if the dog is ready to go through these emotions, through the pain, he can cross the boundary, and the current stops, and then, finally, the collar stops vibrating after crossing these invisible boundaries. Then, he has crossed into a new, unlimited world.

What unpleasant feeling surfaces when you get closer to your dreams or closer to deciding to start creating what you have been wanting to create?

If you are ready to always allow your energy to flow in and out, instead of hanging on to it and creating energy clogs, and if you are willing to go through the pain, to walk through your invisible fence of fear, then you have arrived into a whole new unlimited world, just like the dog. Opportunities start presenting themselves, and your dreams start to come true. All of a sudden, you have 100 new dreams to start following to make them manifest into your reality. If you are willing to start experiencing and enjoying it all — the bad and the wildly awesome — then, things start to happen for you.

You are going to stop blocking your energy and hanging on to the emotional patterns that resurface on a regular basis and stop you.

Knowing that the discomfort is only temporary, does that have an impact on you, before you make the next decision?

Allow yourself to be the freaking awesome human being you are in any situation from now on.

Wow, I have a bruise, and I am loving it. I feel so alive today.

IT'S ALL ABOUT YOUR PERSPECTIVE.

You have an amazing outlook on life, and you being here right now reading this book is proof of that. You are absolutely taking the right steps in your life right now. You are making all the right moves to grow. You are absolutely doing great things with your life right now, and you can feel it.

Have you heard about someone or do you know someone who has loads of natural talents, but they are being wasted or taken for granted?

Most of us know someone or have heard of someone like that.

Can I inform you of something important right now?

You can say yes out loud, now!

The same principle applies to you, if you're going to learn all these processes and methods that you have been learning in this book and everything you learn on your own, if you're not going to use any of it.

None of the coaching is going to work, unless you start using it, unless you start practicing and taking action.

IT DOES NOT MATTER WHAT YOU KNOW, IF YOU ARE NOT USING IT.

Take my advice, I am not using it (just joking). You can smile now, lol. It's not that serious, is it?

One of the best slogans of all times and very relevant here, is the Nike slogan, just do it! It applies to everything you learn, just do it!

What excuses have you been using to avoid taking any action on, what you already have the knowledge to perform?

It does not matter how good the excuses are, there are a lot of things we simply don't do. But why?

Is it too much hassle?

That's nonsense. Have you ever had to take out the trash when you didn't feel like it, but the trash was already starting to smell bad? Have you had to change a full diaper of number two and it's smells awful?

It's likely that you have had to do one or the other at some point, or that you had to do something else that you did not want to do. You probably didn't jump up and down yelling:

I'm so lucky, this will be fun!

No, probably not, but you know what? You did it anyway. To start moving towards your goals and dreams, you will have to do some things with that same attitude you used when you took out the trash. You just did it. So, just starting doing it! Just do it!

> **You will surprise yourself when you allow yourself to see how much energy is within you right now.**

Here's a quick example to prove that you have unlimited energy at your call, with the right mindset.

You are head-over-heels in love, and you barely need to sleep, nor eat. You are filled with energy. Then, one day, out of the blue, your boyfriend or girlfriend dumps you. You are shocked, and now, you have a broken heart. Everything becomes extremely difficult, and you completely shut down. You have no energy. You order pizza, so you don't have to leave the house. Three weeks later, with a filthy house, a text message pops up on your phone. The text message is from you ex, about how stupid she was and that letting you go was the biggest mistake ever, and she is still madly in love with you. The moment you finish reading the message, you light up from within. You become energetic. Your ex asks if she can come over and see you. You jump into the shower, dress up, and clean the whole house in less than an hour. Now, you are full of energy and joy.

Do you relate in any way to this story?

What's going on here?

Where did that energy come from?

Yes, that's right: from within you. You have it in you right now, and you can unleash it whenever you want. When you start to see the solutions in life and love more. When you stop creating energy blocks, and stop being a victim, you will have an endless source of energy within you. When you think you just can't do it, you are right, because you chose to believe that. When you think you can, then you are also right.

YOU ARE AN UNLIMITED SOURCE OF ENERGY.

When you realize that you are the witness behind your feelings, experiences, and thoughts, you shift into the fifth gear in your spiritual growth. Your growth has no limits when you start allowing yourself to go through the pain and allow the pain to come in and go back out with ease and when you start to enjoy all the experiences that you get to experience, the good and the bad.

How will your life be, when you experience everything in the present moment and enjoy the experience (of course, some experiences hurt — I mean being in the now and going through it) without resurfacing old emotional patterns you have been holding on to?

Did you know that you can see past the faults in others and never again be bothered by the shortcomings of others?

I'm not kidding. It is possible to live your life, so that you will never be irritated by anything that others do. Others cannot make you feel happy or sad, the only person who can do that is you. Imagine your life today, if you live as the witness and you start to enjoy experiencing everything in the NOW, letting every experience come in and back out with ease. Enjoy getting to experience a broken heart, to feel sorrow and joy and, of course, all the other beautiful happy experiences, as well.

Putting this in perspective, let's say that when you wake up tomorrow morning, there is an angel who comes and says to you,

I want you to enjoy this day to the fullest, because tonight, when you go to sleep, I will come to take you home. This is your last day.

Imagine: how is your day going to be?

How will you treat your family?

How will you show your love to anyone you meet tomorrow?

How good will the food taste?

How likely are you to become upset over the behavior of others?

How would you do things differently?

Or maybe the biggest question is: what would you do tomorrow?

Would this be one of your best days ever?

Isn't it likely, knowing that it's your last day?

Now, answer this question. Would you be doing the same things you are doing today, if you knew this was your last day?

If your answer is that you would be doing exactly the same things you are doing today and that you would treat your people exactly the same, then, you are doing incredible things with your life right now. You are where most of us would like to be at. If you are currently living your life and loving everything that you get to experience, if you are talking to your people every day, like it's your last, you are absolutely totally freaking awesome and someone to look up to.

If you are not, ask yourself: what's stopping you from starting right now, today?

What is it that's stopping you from releasing all the old emotional patterns you hold onto and block your energy flow?

It's enough to decide right now to start noticing everything and consciously become the witness. Let go of everything you've decided to hold onto from your past, including good experiences — it's not good to hang on to any kind of experience and block your energy flow. Letting go and not hanging on, is not the same as forgetting, just to be clear.

Now, it's time to take a deep breath in, and then, let it go back out with force, counting backwards from five. Stay alert each time an old emotional pattern resurfaces, and use this method to slowly but surely let go of all the energy blocks as they surface. The next time you see that car, smell that smell, hear that song, see your ex, and those old emotional patterns pops up, enjoy letting it go for good. The more you can let in and out, the better your energy flows between your chakras, and the more likely your health will last, way longer than it will with energy blocks. Even though we are not allowed to state that the flow of energy heals you, there are countless examples, in books, studies, articles, and videos that confirm that, but it is always entirely up to you what you decide to believe and what you are willing to implement into your reality.

As always, I encourage you to do your own research and read as much as possible about the subject, if you are in doubt.

Before completing this chapter, practice releasing an energy block. Take a deep breath in, and fill your lungs completely. Blow the air back out with force, and count backwards from five, and let go.

Do this now!

Well done, how was that? Did that feel good?

Imagine how good that will feel when you actually release that unwanted old emotional pattern.

ARE YOU SMILING?

You can smile now, because this was just the beginning of things to come. You are freaking awesome. This was you letting go of something you were holding on to. Fantastic super amazing.

Now, be completely in the present moment, and feel how powerful and pure the flow of energy is in your body right here and right now.

20

PURPOSE

> *Welcome back to the book on this beautiful day. Yes, no matter what the weather is like, this day is beautiful.*

Did you already decide that this day would be a good day?

If not, why not?

Anything that you decide is a thousand times more likely to come true. In case you did not decide yet, simply decide now! This will be an awesome time reading this chapter, and the rest of this day will be exceptionally great. That's right and you know it!

It's all about the change within you that controls whether this day will be great or not. There is nothing that changes outside of you — well, yes, maybe people who you influence change, but not things, debt, the hole in the roof, or the hole in your back pocket of your pants from keeping your phone there. It is all about the change you make within yourself and how you look at things, your perspective and how you experience the events of this day. By you deciding that this be a great day, you can change a lot of things. It can easily have the effect on you that your brain sends out happy hormones, instead of stress hormones under the same circumstances. The change happened because you changed your view of things by deciding it. After you start spreading the feel-good hormones throughout your body, you start to influence other people around you in a positive way, and then, you have managed to make this day even better. It could potentially have the effects on someone that he or she would offer to repair the hole in your roof, because it is such a wonderful feeling being around your happiness hormones that emanate from you like a care-bear stare.

Being around happy people, being around you, feels so good. Well done! Now, you are allowed to put up that irresistible smile I've been hearing about. Yes, that's right, go ahead and put up a huge smile right now, no matter how hard or easy you feel life is right now.

SMILE!

That was absolutely fantastic. With that smile, you just made this day a little bit better. Well done!

After this chapter, later on today, take some time out for yourself, and find out what your purpose is. If you've done this exercise before, it will not take long at all, this time around. You can do it in your head this time or write it down on paper again, which, of course, always works better. If this is the first time you do this exercise, it is important that you schedule a 20 to 40-minute time slot later today, this evening, or wake up earlier tomorrow morning and do it.

Find yourself a quiet place, where you will not be bothered while you write down on a piece paper everything you love to do, everything that brings you joy. Write down a word or a sentence that represents a time when you are your happiest, again and again, line after line, and put a number before each line, whether it is a single word or phrase in the line. You may need to write down 40 to 160 lines, or even more, before you get that A-HA moment that this exercise is all about. It's very important that you do not quit, until you get that A-HA moment. When you feel that A-HA moment, when you see that something is emerging again and again, it's exactly what your purpose is — or at least very close to it.

This could be teaching, traveling, showing love, writing, organizing, composing something, making people laugh, giving people an experience, or helping people out. This is something that gives you greater joy than anything else in life.

When you experience that A-HA moment, it's up to you to give it more attention in your life and see how you can do more of this. You know, this thing you now know is your purpose. Do not worry, no matter what pattern emerges, you will gradually move closer to living your life with purpose on purpose, by doing more of this thing, that triggers this enormous emotional ecstasy within you. Your purpose can change somewhat on your journey, and that is absolutely great, because you are always growing, and that is one of the reasons why you do these exercises more often that just once. When you purposely start doing more of what gives you this unique emotional joy and love, more brilliant things, opportunities, and people start appearing in your reality.

With your purpose in mind, use this question to help guide yourself into creating a plan to start living more purposefully:

How will my actions improve people's lives?

Light and darkness are opposites — or are they? That's what most of us were taught, anyway.

What is darkness, anyway?

Is it something that really exists?

Darkness is a place where there is no light. Darkness is not the opposite of light, but something without light.

Love is associated with something good, and when we talk about something bad or evil, it is not the opposite of good, it's something without love. Your brain is dependent on creating opposites, left and right, up and down, to understand things better, while your heart can understand the purity of light and love without an opposite. That is why we say that when you create something with your brain, you automatically create the opposite of what you are creating, at the same time, no matter how good your intentions are.

> ***When you create with your heart, you create without opposites. Pure creation!***

You've probably heard many times something like, he is in his heart when he works with children, or she is so heart-centered when she is painting, or anything that refers to operating directly from the heart — it is pure creation, without the opposites.

Some people talk about and/or to, the universe, others talk about God, and some about the energy, and others about the source. What all these have in common is that they are talking about the same thing. People just use different names.

Many people who are believers, and I am specifically talking about Christians, believe that there is a hell. But most of us know that it does not exist, at least not as we were told to believe it from the Bible. The Bible was written by humans, and the brain must have opposites to understand things. If anything could possibly be close to being hell, it would be in this existence, but it is not so. The concept of hell was created by men centuries ago, as a tool to control the masses, to be able to threaten them and tell them that if they do not do this or that, then, they go to this terrible place.

If it is true that the creator created man with free will, why would he create a place to punish man for the wrong choices?

Does anyone have free will who is punished every time she chooses wrong, until she finally chooses what the creator had decided she should choose all along and then, finally she gets rewarded?

There is no hell, although man has created the concept of hell as a scare tactics management tool a long time ago. It does not matter whether you believe in a certain religion or not for the content in the chapter, or in this book for that matter. Most religions in the world are trying to explain the same truth, with the interpretation of the men and women who wrote the books, based on their experience, their culture, and their lives. There is truth in all religions, but the interpretation of man is something that makes this complicated and does not age very well. If you would write yet another book today trying to explain your human experience to the creator, it would also become obsolete, after some time, because it is describing the human experience of the person who wrote the book, to the creator. Humanity is always evolving, and what was true 1,000 years ago, is no longer true for the modern human, all the way down to the DNA level. Humanity is evolving very fast now, faster than ever.

The creator, God — or the energy that we all come from — is pure love. All you must do is love and be love, in order to advance, to reserve your seat on the ride to the next destination, wherever that is. Go to the next level in this video game we are playing, metaphorically speaking about the human experience.

Many people ask the creator or the universe to take something away from them, such as illness, mentality, bad luck, worries, uncertainty, or something that person no longer wants. Let's take a closer look at that.

If you have free will, why should your creator ever take anything from you? He will, on the other hand accept something from you as a gift and he will also assist yourself to heal you, but to take something from you, I don't think so.

If you are at a point where you wish desperately to get rid of something, why not try to give the creator — or the universe — that which you no longer want? If you're someone who prays, how about trying to give the next time, instead of begging for something in the prayer?

Here you go, please take this bad luck as a gift from me, this disease, this lack of energy, or this memory, I have carried this with me long enough to have learned what I needed, to achieve this spiritual growth, and now, I am ready for the next level in my existence here. Here you go, I give this to you now, because I no longer need it, thank you.

What are you worth?

What do you deserve, on a scale from one to one hundred?

If one is to deserve nothing or that this is going so well that soon something must go terribly wrong and 100 is to deserve all the good things and experiences life has to offer, without paying for it in one way or another, like karma.

How do you rate yourself?

Most people will rate themselves somewhere between 50 and 95.

There is a big difference between the things you can influence, and the things that you have complete control over. Life is always about your point of view. Like the story about the three blind men who are describing the elephant. One was touching the trunk, another held onto his leg, and the third held on to his tail. They were all describing the same animal, but the description was so different, based on their perspective, that one might think they were describing three different species.

What is your point of view on life?

What are you worth?

What do you deserve?

We are all equally valuable and deserve all that life has to offer, but, unfortunately, only few know that. I think you are beginning to see that and understand why. Let's suppose that you just ranked yourself as an 85 on the scale. Let's put that number into perspective. When you look at a newborn child and you are asked to value this innocent pure child's worth, do you automatically respond 85?

Lol, no, I am pretty sure that it's probably something more like this:

Oh wow, she's beautiful, and she is definitely worth 100 on the scale. She deserves everything good.

Do you know what?

You are that newborn child!

When did you start to reduce your worth?

You are worth 100 on the scale!

You have a tendency to judge things on the outside, even though you know that no experience takes place outside your body. You are the queen or king, who lives in the castle or palace. Outside the palace is a small city or village, and outside the village are strong walls.

Why do you sometimes think that you are the walls?

You are the queen or king!

You are not these walls, no more than you are your body. The body is just your walls. Your body is your vehicle. You deserve as much today as when you were that newborn child.

You are an incredibly awesome human being, a great being of light, and it's great to be you. Congrats on being you.

GO AHEAD, SMILE!

Feelings and emotions are part of the human experience, and you have no control over them and shouldn't even be trying to be controlling them. They are neither right nor wrong, but what you do have control over is how you show them.

It is okay for you to be angry, but how do you show your anger? You can be angry, noticing it consciously that you are angry, without letting the anger control your actions and taking it out on your environment or other people.

It's okay to get angry, but how you show your feelings? Do you allow your emotional horses to run wildly forward without having your hands on the reins, or can you stay calm long enough to let the anger fade away before attacking someone or breaking something?

Can you enjoy experiencing all these emotions, without allowing your emotions to control you?

You are the controller, and you must put both hands on the reins of your emotional horses that pull your vehicle. There is spiritual growth in learning to control how you steer the horses toward your spiritual growth that you want to experience and aim for.

Do you have your hands on the reins or not?

If not, why not try it?

Why not try to be able to look within and say:

Wow, I'm angry right now!

Then, write a letter while you are angry, and wait until the following morning before doing anything else. Your emotions can have such an impact on you that when you read your thoughts the next day, it's like another person wrote the letter. You should have both your hands on the reins from now on. You are in control, and if you let go of them, you allow your feelings to take control.

Take control, right now!

Well done!

It all starts with a decision.

How you respond to your emotions and show them, is what you control. Humor, for example, is a great way to deal with many emotions. Like the story about the man who went in front of everyone in line at the airport and said,

Give me a first-class ticket, now!

The woman smiled towards him and said to him politely,

"You must go to the back of the line, like everyone else."

The man got angry and said, "Do you know who I am?"

The woman then spoke directly into the intercom system and said with a smile on her face, "Ladies and gentlemen, we have a man at check-in counter who does not know who he is, can anyone in here help us identify the man?"

The man got even angrier, and as he was walking away from the check-in, he said, "Bloody hell."

The woman quickly replied to him once again with a smile,

"If you want us to look for a ticket for you, you must go to the back of the line, sir."

Whether this story is true or not, it is a great example of how to deal with a situation with humor. The woman was probably angry at first, seeing the man rush in front of everyone, but she decided not to react to her feelings, and instead, she responded to the situation by having both hands on her reins and she responded to the situation with humor.

Do you have any characteristic that you do not like today and want to change?

If so, you can step into a role that has all the desired characteristics you wish to acquire.

Let me explain. Let's suppose for a minute that you are an actor, and you get the main role in a play that requires you to play a completely different personality than you are in your daily life. You do not feel good about this in the beginning, because this role is so far from your own personality. Slowly, but surely, you start doing more acting on stage in that character, because everyone loves this character you're playing. Your character is understanding, patient, loving, and wise. You don't display your usual behavior while you are playing this wonderful character. When you are on stage, acting, you can be perfect, because you're just acting, but while you are in the role of this perfect character, all your real feelings are simmering beneath the surface. This perfect character becomes so popular that they start adding new daily performances, and you step into this perfect character more and more each week. It does not take long before you're staying in this perfect character for many hours every day. Even more hours than those that you are yourself — you know, that imperfect, impulsive, bad-tempered, and intolerant person you are or maybe we should say, that you were.

By stepping into this perfect character over and over again, you have managed to have full control of your emotions, which are, by the way, neither right nor wrong. One of the things you have accomplished during this time period is not letting your emotions break out in anger, for example. You have not let your emotions affect other people in a bad way. No, you've gone all-in. When acting on stage, you have stepped all the way into the character and learned to stop reacting to your emotions, and you are showing signs of being a perfectly balanced person while acting.

A year later, you realize that you are no longer reacting to your feelings, and that you are starting to have much better control over how you show your emotions. You know for a fact that you have no control whether the emotions and feelings continue to appear or not, but, now, a few years later, you have complete control over how you show your emotions and how you respond to them. You've seen incredible spiritual growth by stepping into this role. You are not the same, but, yet, you are not another.

This is a very interesting example for you to ponder, and even follow.

If you plan to become a world champion in swimming, chess, or gymnastics, you know it's not going to happen overnight.

The same is true when it comes to your feelings and emotions. Learning not to react, but to respond to them. It takes time to become a master of anything. Your decision to become the world champion in swimming tonight will not manifest overnight; it will take longer than that. The decision to become the world champion in anything is just the first step.

Then, you need to step into the character who has the characteristics needed to achieve the success you desire. You must practice every day to become a champion. You will gradually become a master of that which you practice over and over again, but you must start acting like the champion you see yourself becoming in the future right now.

In this journey we call life, there is only one person who will always be your hardest critic, and it's you.

> **On your journey, there is no one who will ever manage to hurt you as much as you do to yourself when you begin to question the wisdom your journey contains.**

Take a chill pill, and ease up on judging yourself. Start stepping into the character you want to become, and start acting. Look at life as a big theatrical play, and you are the main star. You are absolutely freaking awesome, and you need to know that, if you don't already know that.

Now, bring your attention to the way you are breathing and carrying yourself. Does is show, in the way you breathe and carry yourself, that you are freaking awesome?

Here's a question you should ask yourself as often as you can:

How am I breathing right now? How am I moving my body right now? Am I stiff, or am I moving with grace?

After asking this question, follow this script.

Take a deep breath, open up your shoulders, stretch your head up towards heaven, so that you stretch your spine and gain about a fourth of an inch and walk, so your graceful movements speak out loud these words:

I AM FREAKING AWESOME!

Not bragging, just confidence, resonating self-love, and dignity, because you are freaking awesome!

Now, it's time for you to promise yourself that you will remember to do the exercise to find your purpose later today or first thing tomorrow morning. But before we wrap up this chapter, here is an exercise for you to coordinate your breathing and body movements together.

Let me explain the exercise first and then, you do it on your own. You can do this exercise as often as you like — every day, or just when you remember to do it is fine, too.

This exercise is really powerful. Use your normal walking pace, and start by taking two steps forward on one breath in, during those two steps and then, another two steps as you breathe out. Next you take three steps forward on one breath in, and three more steps on your out breath. Then, go to four steps as you breathe in, and four more steps for your out breath. You get the picture. It's so simple that you can do this exercise in the parking lot walking from the car to the grocery store.

See how high you can get, and when you reach your limit, track back down, as well — 20, 19, 18, and so on. If you get to 20 or more, it is super-amazing, but just do as much as you can for now, and you will get better and better at this, the more you do this exercise.

Go ahead and implement this breath walk into your lifestyle, and remember how incredibly amazing and great you are right here and right now.

BON VOYAGE

Dear reader — yes, you, beautiful soul — thank you so much for purchasing and reading the book **You Are FREAKING AWESOME**. I hope you enjoyed reading this book as much as I enjoyed creating it for you.

I hope you have implemented many of the exercises in this book, and that it will allow you to step into the greatness that awaits you.

You are simply freaking amazing. #Truthbomb

This book is great to have handy to be able to pick up and read a single chapter whenever you need and/or want to.

Stay tuned for the next 20 chapters in the next book, as I keep advancing my teaching methods. I am already two chapters into the sequel as I am finishing the final editing touches on this book before publishing. Thank you so much, beautiful soul.

Sincerely, the author, Huni Hunfjord. I love you. ❤❤

THE AUTHOR, Huni Hunfjord

Titles include:

Sleeping Habits and Routines

Top 1% Parents Raise Top 1% Children

The Mentorian

Our Road without Boundaries

You are FREAKING AWESOME.

I am the founder of the Watchon brand, Focus Gym ❤❤ Be you! and Focus Gym ❤❤ Walk the Talk.

I strive to grow each day and impact as many lives, in a positive way, as I possibly can. I am a parent. I am a student. I am a teacher. I am a coach. I am a music composer. I am a healer, and I am super grateful for you.

I love you.

LEARN MORE ABOUT Huni Hunfjord

Books by Huni Hunfjord
http://amazon.com/author/HuniHunfjord
http://www.lulu.com/spotlight/HuniHunfjord

Huni Hunfjord's website
http://HuniHunfjord.com

Learn more about Focus Gym ❤❤ Be you!
http://FocusGymBeyou.com

Learn more about Focus Gym ❤❤ Walk the Talk
http://FocusGymWalktheTalk.com

Jabez Orphanage Spirit School of Excellence
http://Jabez.HuniHunfjord.com

One Last Thing...

If you enjoyed this book or found it entertaining or educational at all, I'd be very grateful if you'd post a short review on Amazon. Your support really does make a difference, and I read all the reviews personally, so I can get your feedback, so I can make this book and the next one even better.

If you'd like to leave a review, all you need to do is review this book on its author's page on Amazon here:

http://amazon.com/author/HuniHunfjord

If you have purchased a printed copy of the book, please send your review directly to testimonial@hunihunfjord.com, as I would love to include your review on my website.

Thanks again for your support, and remember that you are freaking awesome and that I love you.

Light and love, Huni Hunfjord. ❤❤

www.ingramcontent.com/pod-product-compliance
Lightning Source LLC
LaVergne TN
LVHW021332080526
838202LV00003B/150